Y0-ELA-503

WITHDRAWN

GARLAND FOR
THE WINTER SOLSTICE

Ruthven Todd

——◦◉◦——

Garland for the Winter Solstice

SELECTED POEMS

An Atlantic Monthly Press Book

LITTLE, BROWN AND COMPANY

BOSTON   TORONTO

ATLANTIC-LITTLE, BROWN BOOKS
ARE PUBLISHED BY
LITTLE, BROWN AND COMPANY
IN ASSOCIATION WITH
THE ATLANTIC MONTHLY PRESS

Printed in Great Britain

Contents

[viii]

[ix]

[x]

SOME of these poems appeared in my earlier collections: *Until Now* (Fortune Press, London, 1942), *The Acreage of the Heart* (McLellan, Glasgow, 1943), *The Planet in my Hand* (Grey Walls Press, London, 1946) and *A Mantelpiece of Shells* (Bonacio & Saul with Grove Press, New York, 1954). Acknowledgements are due to the publishers of these books.

I would also like to thank the editors of the various periodicals in which poems were first printed and, for nostalgic reasons (since some of them are no longer with us), I list as many as I can now recall, in alphabetical order: *American Scholar, Art News, Botteghe Oscure, Contemporary Poetry & Prose, Furioso, Here & Now* (Toronto), *Horizon, Kingdom Come, Life & Letters Today, The Listener, London Bulletin, London Magazine, Modern Reading, Nation, New Verse, Now, Poems for Spain, Poetry* (Chicago), *Poetry* (London), *Poetry* (Scotland), *Poetry Quarterly, Programme, Scottish Bookman, Some Poems in War-time, T. S. Eliot; A Symposium, Twentieth Century Verse, Vineyard Gazette, Windmill*. I trust that any omissions will be forgiven me.

'Northern New Jersey: Near Warwick, New York,' 'A Mantelpiece of Shells,' 'Garland for the Winter Solstice,' and 'The Hawk's Victim' appeared originally in *The New Yorker*.

As the poems are not arranged in a strictly chronological order, I have given the places and dates of composition in parentheses in the list of contents to avoid cluttering the pages with extraneous matter.

Elegy

Nostalgic for a world I never knew
I have no wish to follow those who
Found that History's borders were not wide
Enough to preserve secure the anonymity,
Those who, the legends say, have never died—
Who never faltered and had not heard of pity.

O Love, I would ask little of tomorrow
If, for today, I could forget the sorrow
Of the unnamed; those, alas, for whom
No verdict is expected, in that hour
When History's jury is informed by Time,
'Consider the fortunate, forget the poor.'

I have seen Hate upon the mountain
With arms upreached above tormented Spain,
Above China, where the uncounted flood
Does not remember the careful acre, the rice
And the fat-bellied children, where blood
Is cheap, and no man worth a bullet's price.

History will not weep for shattered Europe.
At twenty now the boy falls smartly into step,
To die or else to kill, while, outside, his world
Runs like a crazy dog, baying for sweet Death
Who will not, if he please, neglect the gnarled
Fingers of the old, or the tangled lovers on the heath

Our world is Whymper on the Matterhorn
Who at the summit saw a legend born

And now feels himself shrivel like the rope
Whipped back towards him from the edge; the four
Crashing among the foothill boulders will not escape
His memory forever. Happy once before

He's had his fill of death and cannot rest.
His own death would be, perhaps, the best
Of any; but the tough fibre of living drives
Him to other ranges, south of the equator,
To conquer Andes, to throw his soul from cliffs;
Cantankerous as a bitch, the unwilling hater.

Our world today is Marius at Carthage
Among the ruins of an unfortunate age;
Our world is Rome gone mad for greater glory,
Greece in the decline, and this our land
Preserving intact the obvious delicious story
To puzzle those who cannot understand.

O Love, recall especially the monstrous lies;
Reject the hand of Hate, the invitation of his eyes.

Imagination

Previously imagination had supplied the details;
The crying wonder of the bomb as flower,
Petalled with flame, and the deep pure red
Of blood, staining the rubble on the parquet floor,
Even the haphazard tracery of tangled entrails
Arranged across the white sheets of a solitary bed.

However, it is not fresh nor clean like this:
Three days have shrunk the lips that once would kiss—
Teeth still are pearls but gums are oyster-flesh,
Will not entice the enquiring tongue of lover;
And over all, this dust, the pall of shabbiness,
Drives out the memory of clay's endeavour.

This boy was Love, who once beside the river
Would wander, free of Time's charmed circle, arm,
Slow inches of his manhood, round another:
Today this boy is Death—rose-trellised broken walls
Are comfortless to those who scared the small alarms
of childhood, whose future here is lost forever. . . .

In Edinburgh 1940

I

Now, O let lovers lie close near Cramond Brig
And the children gather the frail clams beside Hound Point,
Beside the little island with the wooden beacon.
O let the summer ripen the clustered rowans,
And the fronds of bracken curl over the Pentland Hills.
Though the May Island be blinded by war, let the fish
Run through the booms, and the Forth break to the sea.

Under the lion-crouching shadow of Arthur's Seat,
Let me walk by the ruined palace, in the vision of history.
Let me walk by the volcanic rock, basalt crowned with the
    Castle,
In Charlotte Square let me hear Sir Walter Scott droning,
Drivelling a dream of history, and let me meet Burns,
Outside the Tron Bar, drunk with disgust as much as
    whisky:

In time of war let me ask him the expected questions—
Ask whether his rocks have melted with the sun
This summer, and whether the tides have all gone dry
Along the Ayrshire coast. O let me observe his distaste
For my cigarettes and half-pint of beer, my snigger of sex.
O do not leave me alone with the ghosts of the past.

II

I was born in this city of grey stone and bitter wind,
Of tenements sooted up with lying history:
This place where dry minds grow crusts of hate, as rocks

Grow lichens. I went to school over the high bridge
Fringed with spikes which, curiously, repel the suicides;
And I slept opposite the rock-garden where the survivors,
Who had left Irving and Mallory under the sheet of snow,
Planted the incarvillea and saxifrages of the Himalayas.

And, as I grew in childhood, I learned the knack to slip
The breech-block of the field-gun in the park, peering
Along the rifled barrel I would enclose a small circle
Of my world, marked out for death; death as unreal
As the gun's forgotten action under the hot African sun.
Growing older, I met other and more frequent ghosts,
Lying to preserve the remnants of a reputation.

Knox spoke sweetly in the Canongate—'I was not cruel
To gaunt Mary, the whore denying the hand that lit the
    fuse.'
Charles Stuart returned, alive only to the past, his venture
That was little but a dream, forgetting the squat bottle,
Quivered in the lace-veined hand and the unseeing sharp-
    ness of his eyes.
Bruce could not stir the cobwebs from his skeleton,
And the editor spoke regretfully, but firmly, of poor Keats.

Here the boy Rimbaud paused, flying love and lust,
Unnoticed on his journey to the Abyssinian plains
And the thick dropsy of his tender leg. Here the other
    Knox,
Surgeon and anatomist, saw the beauty of the young girl
Smothered by Burke and Hare. And here, O certainly,
God was the private property of a chosen few
Whose lives ran carefully and correctly to the grave.

This, deny it as I like, is still my city and these ghosts,
Sneer as I may, have helped to make me what I am.
A woman cried in labour and Simpson inhaled his vapour
Falling, anaesthetized, across the drawing-room table.
John Graham, laird of Claverhouse, did not have tears
For those he killed, nor did the silver bullet weep for him.
This city, bulwark of the east wind, formed me as I am.

III

I am the Crusoe of my heart, lord of the vagus nerve,
John seeing the sixth seal opened and the curtain of blood
Shuttering my mind, Simon, perched on the twin columns
Of my legs, St. Lawrence roasted on the gridiron of my
    skeleton.
I am Christ crucified upon the cross-bow of my ribs.

I was the boy following Childe Harold up the Rhine,
Who saw Cortez conquer Mexico and the golden sun
Overthrown, who slept beside the Martello tower
To watch the beacons flare, from Kent to Cumberland;
Who saw Richthofen, dead, land safely on the earth.

O I was these in dreams, and in my shadow I detect
Their shapes. Their hands grapple and fingers point
From the trees in the public parks, and they accuse
Me always. They are the masters of my failure
And can cover me with the green darkness of their night.

'Remember,' the universal voice speaks, 'the Flaming
    Mountain,
My River of Ice that would not cool my Burns,
The Revelation on Patmos and the Footprint in the Sand,
Remember, O can you forget? Napoleon: that Winter
Of Snow and Fire; the Rocking Horse on the Island.

Remember Trelawny removing the specially fashioned
   Boot,
To find as he desired, the Cloven Hoof, and that small Hill
Shaped like a Skull, and the dead Hands on the Pilot's
Stick.
O recall these Things, for they, also, were a Part;
They were the Milky Way of Dreams, Hoops to your
   Mind's Staves.'

IV

Now I ask love from the stars in a time of hate
And, also, beg peace from the voice of the dead.
I cannot, however much I desire it, deny the past.
What, I say to the midsummer moon, can I do in this
   city,
And where can I walk to avoid the lies of history?

From my place here, beside the cemetery where the
   poisoner
Hid his evidence, I walk among the cities of the weeping
   world;
Stumble among the ruins of Madrid and lean on the frame-
   work
That once was Warsaw, look at Oslo and Copenhagen,
And at that latest city, Paris, where dreams were tough as
   steel.

O in this bright summer of a breaking world
I write these lines as a memorial to this city,
This outpost, one of many, of my ingenuous heart,
Remembering its history as a pile of trash
And its teaching false as the light of a dead star.

O the green walnut of my heart is hard and dry
On this occasion devoted to the repertory of death:
I remark that the lying legend of this town
Makes no concession to those who are alive.
This city, truant of time, is lost, alas, in history.

Che Farò Senza Euridice?

Look upward, darling, at the umpteen million stars,
And at the Plough's blue furrow to beyond the Pole,
And think how once—forget the embittered years—
Love was your life and so you could not fail.

Sweet, I would ask you if your secret cave
Grew flowers of mica or of quartz to compensate
For the shallow bowl of rock above your curls? The grave,
We are informed, is narrow, dark and wet,

And the wood-walled heritage of the dead
Falls into mould and clay, no pillared stalagmite
Launches itself between the soft bones; the head
Is empty as a rotten nut. Look at the stars tonight,

And weep for all the things that now are past,
Let your tears drown the planets; the lonely dog
Yelps its protest for the murdered moon, lost
In the smothering coy embraces of the acid fog.

Love once was a game, a contest just like life,
And death was the same silver cup for either side.
Remember Orpheus turning: 'O my beautiful, the knife
Of hell has whittled down my easy stride!'

Remember the unidentifiable flowers nodding
At the entrance of the cave, and the few birds'
Inquisitive peering and the little clouds of cotton-wadding;
And your return—carrying a hundredweight of words.

Dear, what do you look for in this hell, where Hope
Died young, and where, indeed, there is no God
To comfort these continents of Asia and Europe;
And even the bright stars cannot make you glad?

The Credulous Boy

for S.S.

O innumerable are the eyes of the unfortunate,
Like withered cornflowers in the field of night;
And the credulous boy walks alone in the city
By the rivers of blood and the towers of tears,
Meeting horrors at corners and death on the stairs
That spiral from the Tube, and the sweep's sooty
Face holds more of terror than the tales relate.

Under the dome of silence where once Marx sat
Until the ideas came out of the books and fought
In his mind, he sits and the image of the poet
Sprouts like an autumn crocus in his cupped hands.
The boy weeps, left alone among history's tombstones
He listens always for the sound of death and the dry throat
Clicking its last message. And the time is late.

In Spain the dust now creeps forever over the bones,
And the Austrian artery flows from the dry mountains,
And the streets weep in China; the Abyssinian maid
Is forgotten. This is our day, day of the Heinkel and the
    mine
With the magnetic horns, of the dead star, of the shrine
Of ten thousand dying Christs and gods who paid
Their debts to hating history. Roll back the stones

And you will find the tombs empty as a drum:
But, O alas, it is not the dead only who are dumb,
For the hurt eyes cannot speak to the Northern Lights,

Or ask favours from the seven planets in the skies;
Voiceless as the giraffe, the unlucky one often cries
And makes no noise; he is the captive of the Menin Gates
And Cenotaphs, he is the Unknown Warrior whose thumb

Was gnawed in agony down to the white knuckle,
He is the shot widgeon whose green neck-hackle
Lay for a winter on the drifted cliff of snow.
Turn your eyes to the wall and read its surface—
The map of the future, the Roman road and the place
Where Styx is dammed with rock and where the flow
Of love sinks from a spate to an uneasy trickle.

Whoever walks often in this city of frantic dreams,
Where millions of the unhappy have made their homes
And where the forgotten are the stones in the street,
Must remember the clock and its twelve points of love,
The understanding glance and the hand that would forgive;
Remember the boy beaten by the avalanche of night,
And the betraying cockerels with their apoplectic combs.

Henry Fuseli

Friendly with few whom the timid state admired
His bitter tongue as frightening as his paint,
Loving Satan, abhoring the overrighteous saint,
In his lifetime he became a legend, non aspired
To equal him in shrewishness or hate.

Appearance—wizened, a teddy-bear with passion,
He spoke his mind when such was not the fashion,
Living to die in bed, twenty years too late.

Yet, though his elders and contemporaries quailed,
His pupils loved him, fondled his advice,
Called his tongue triumphant, though his brush failed
To oust the masters from their envied place.
His words still sparkle from a thousand letters,
Dimming the lustre wit of those Time called his betters.

William Blake

Such balance of perfection few had dared,
The morning stars sang evenly and sweet
And those who lectured, sneered or stared
Forgot the whole world lying beneath his feet.

Inevitably, the fury of his course upset
The amiable poet riding by the sea;
Those who believed could only but regret
So very few saw angels in a tree.

When in the end the giants of Albion strode
Along the pillared heights of Primrose Hill,
All Eden's fruits were his, nothing the gods forbade,
Death could not count his riches in the till.

Despite his errors he was bound to win,
Knowing no good could flourish without sin.

In Memoriam: My Father
29 April, 1944

Shut in his frosty valley at the Northern fringe of time,
Beyond the tundra and the ever-howling wolves,
The hours went slowly by, the minutes knocking lame,
As sixty summers lay counted on his shelves.

A life ebbed slowly down the Solway of its years,
Forgetting the floods of youth, the tides that swept
More cruel in their intensity than all the heartfelt tears
Which stained the linen pillow on which the dreamer slept.

The lock-gates of the life he always loved
Could still withstand the batterings of disease,
Despite Death's mathematics which had often proved
Himself the one physician to bring perfect ease.

Now I, lying all these hundred miles to south,
Can think of him dispassionately, with pity;
Recalling tonight the weak but usually kindly mouth,
The mind that shuddered from the world's immensity;

Recalling the man whose universe was sometimes shut
Within the unmeasured boundaries of a postage-stamp;
The man for whom the mellow whisky could garotte
The marchers of history with their metronomic tramp;

The man who built as strong as man could build
Yet saw, before his end, how bricks and concrete fell away
As the destiny he always feared was finally fulfilled
And all the horror of his youth again held sway.

This man, as complex as an antique clock,
Was my own father whom I cannot see quite round;
I work all night and yet my portraits lack
Those final touches which would show I understand

The man as man, divorced from being only me,
Copying my own image in an eternal mirror:
The facts which others now report can only be
The distortions caused by my inevitable error.

When last I saw him, lying uneasy on his bed,
I knew that I at length had grown to be a man,
For all my rancours and my fears were dead;
I saw him once again as when my memory began.

And it is thus I hope I will remember him;
Before his share of the world's apple proved too sour,
Before his dreams of greatness loomed too dim
In the haze which helped to pass the intolerable hour.

I would remember him as the man who drew
With coloured chalks upon my childhood's page,
The witch from whom no small boy ever flew,
The friendly troll, the ogre who had hardly any rage.

So to his memory, I dedicate these lines,
Dumb with a feeling I cannot now express;
Glad that, at least, the heartache which remains
Instead of hating has learned how to bless.

Watching You Walk

Watching you walk slowly across a stage,
Suddenly I am become aware of all the past;
Of all the tragic maids and queens of every age,
Of Joan, whose love the flames could not arrest.

Of those to whom always love was the first duty,
Who saw behind the crooked world the ugly and weak,
Whose kindliness was no gesture; no condescending pity
Could rule their actions; those whom Time broke,

But whom he could not totally destroy.
Hearing the truth you give to these dead words,
Whose writer feared the life they might enjoy,
I can recall the mating orchestra of birds

Behind your voice, as lying by the lake,
You read me Owen, and I, too deeply moved,
Watched the swans for a moment, before I spoke
The trivialities, unable to tell you how I loved.

Watching your fingers curl about a painted death,
I am suddenly glad that it is April, that you are queen
Of all the sordid marches of my bruised heart,
That, loving you, the poplars never seemed so green;

Glad of my lonely walk beside the shrunken river,
Thinking of you while seeing the tufts of ash,
The chestnut candles and unreal magnolia's wax flower;
Glad that, in loving you, the whole world lives afresh.

Various Ends

Sidney, according to report, was kindly hearted
　　When stretched upon the field of death;
And in his gentleness, ignored the blood that spurted,
　　Expending the last gutter of his flickering breath.

Marlowe, whose raw temper used to rise
　　Like boiling milk, went on the booze;
A quick word and his half-startled eyes
　　Mirrored his guts flapping on his buckled shoes.

Swift went crazy in his lonely tower,
　　Where blasphemous obscenity paid the warders,
Who brought a string of visitors every hour
　　To see the wild beast, the Dean in holy orders.

And there were those coughed out their sweet soft lungs
　　Upon the mountains, or the clear green sea.
Owen found half-an-ounce of lead with wings;
　　And Tennyson died quietly, after tea.

Sam Johnson scissored at the surgeon's stitches
　　To drain more poison from his bloated body.
And Byron may have recalled the pretty bitches,
　　Nursing his fevered head in hands unsteady.

De Nerval finished swinging from a grid
　　And round his neck the Queen of Sheba's garter.
Swinburne died of boredom, doing as he was bid,
　　And Shelley bobbed lightly on the Mediterranean water.

Rimbaud, his leg grown blue and gross and round,
  Lay sweating for these last weeks on his truckle-bed;
He could not die—the future was unbroken ground—
  Only Paris, Verlaine and poetry were dead.

Blake had no doubts, his old fingers curled
  Around dear Kate's frail and transparent hand;
Death merely meant a changing of his world,
  A widening of experience, it marked no end.

The Truth in the Bottle

Two at a table talking in the mirrored room,
Watching the cradled bottle run down towards its dregs,
Two of the woof on the world's vast loom,
Watching their lives shuttle as the evening goes.

The old tune that the band plays is a shuffled card,
We are the master-tellers of this fortunate game,
And as the bottle shrinks are slightly off our guard,
Risking, in confidence, our hearts upon a name;

Always and forever, our inevitable guesses are right,
An invisible audience gives us its fond applause,
Bowing, we hesitate, caught in a sudden fright,
For these were the names we mention to ourselves.

Should others hear of them now would the spell break
And the unhoped-for deliverance come to pass?
Drink deep, my sweet, for the truth you seek
May meet with my truth at the bottom of a glass.

Sit, watch the world spin to our respective places;
Nothing now hurts in the scenes the heart revisits,
Yet something quails before the stern or cruel faces,
And for a moment our own quiet hells we savour.

O I shall remember the beautiful witch in the corner,
When I was one of a pair in the mirrored room,
When my shyness was more than the truth in the bottle,
But less than my happiness glowing in the gloom.

Against the Adversary

When fortunate Hector came at length
To meet the foul adversary face to face,
He found he could dictate no terms
To one whose currency was worms,
Whose mansion was so narrow a place,
With vapours that would vanquish strength.

The emperors of the world's estate,
Attila and Genghis Khan both found,
Was shallower than they'd ever thought,
Not all their riches could have bought
So very rare a piece of ground,
Damp-stained and cold and maculate;

And all the lordly heard the weevil
Dining at ease upon the proudest heart,
The maggot savour marrow's succulence,
Hold triumph over tyrant's truculence
As the flaked flesh fell silently apart,
And the mind knew naught of good or evil.

Dear heart, the obsessions of the grave
Permit us little time to demonstrate
Faithful intent or well-kept vow,
Nor will they ever show us how
To beat the adversary who beat the great,
In whose dominions king is slave.

If to her love-lost limbo Eurydice fell
By virtue of her singer's brave desire
Who heard the worm work at its loom
And turned to save her from the tomb,
Casting away the guardian lyre:
Surely these two be spared from hell?

Revenge

Following a cruel winter with hard sudden frosts
The old man died. His sons who had neglected
Him so long found less than they'd expected—
Advice and an old chart the sum of his bequests.
This plan was neatly plotted to a careful scale,
And showed where, near half the world away,
Treasure was hidden on a summer's day
By one who sacked a city for its spoil.

The brothers met great trouble with their ship,
Encountered waterspouts and twisted fishes
That were to them the emblems of lost hope,
For, when they dug, they saw no hidden riches,
Nothing but lugworms in the shifting sand—
Which was exactly as the old man planned.

Personal History

for my son

O my heart is the unlucky heir of the ages
And my body is unwillingly the secret agent
Of my ancestors; those content with their wages
From history: the Cumberland Quaker whose gentle
Face was framed with lank hair to hide the ears
Cropped as a punishment for his steadfast faith,
The Spanish lady who had seen the pitch lake's broth
In the West Indian island and the Fife farmers
To whom the felted barley meant a winter's want.

My face presents my history, and its sallow skin
Is parchment for the Edinburgh lawyer's deed:
To have and hold in trust, as feoffee therein
Until such date as the owner shall have need
Thereof. My brown eyes are jewels I cannot pawn,
And my long lip once curled beside an Irish bog,
My son's whorled ear was once my father's, then mine;
I am the map of a campaign, each ancestor has his flag
Marking an advance or a retreat. I am their seed.

As I write I look at the five fingers of my hand,
Each with its core of nacre bone, and rippled nails;
Turn to the palm and the traced unequal lines that end
In death—only at the tips my ancestry fails—
The dotted swirls are original and are my own:
Look at this fringed polyp which I daily use
And ask its history, ask to what grave abuse
It has been put: perhaps it curled about the stone
Of Cain. At least it has known much of evil,

And perhaps as much of good, been tender
When tenderness was needed, and been firm
On occasion, and in its past been free of gender,
Been the hand of a mother holding the warm
Impress of the child against her throbbing breast,
Been cool to the head inflamed in fever,
Sweet and direct in contact with a lover.
O in its cupped and fluted shell lies all the past;
My fingers close about the crash of history's storm.

In the tent of night I hear the voice of Calvin
Expending his hatred of the world in icy words;
Man less than a red ant beneath the towering mountain,
And God a troll more fearful than the feudal lords;
The Huguenots in me, flying Saint Bartholomew's Day,
Are in agreement with all this, and their resentful hate
Flames brighter than the candles on an altar, the grey
Afternoon is lit by Catherine Wheels of terror, the street
Drinks blood and pity is death before their swords.

The cantilever of my bones acknowledges the architect,
My father, to whom always the world was a mystery
Concealed in the humped base of a bottle, one solid fact
To set against the curled pages and the tears of history.
I am a Border keep, a croft and a solicitor's office,
A country rectory, a farm and a drawing-board:
In me, as in so many, the past has stored its miser's hoard,
Won who knows where nor with what loaded dice.
When my blood pulses it is their blood I feel hurry.

These forged me, the latest link in a fertile chain
With ends that run so far that my short sight
Cannot follow them, nor can my weak memory claim
Acquaintance with the earliest shackle. In my height

And breadth I hold my history, and then my son
Holds my history in his small body and the history of
  another,
Who for me has no contact but that of flesh, his mother.
What I make now I make, indeed, from the unknown,
A blind man spinning furiously in the web of night.

Delusion of Grandeur

From a strange land among the hills, the tall man
Came; who was a cobbler and a rebel at the start
Till he saw power ahead and keenly fought
To seize it; crushed out his comrades then.
His brittle eyes could well outstare the eagle
And the young followed him with cheers and praise,
Until, at last, all that they knew—his nights, his days,
His deeds and face were parcel of a fable.

Now in the neat white house that is his home
He rules the birds and flowers like a king,
Napoleon by the sundial, sees his fame
Spread through the garden to the heap of dung:
'All that I do is history,' he cries,
Seeing in his shadow his romantic size.

16 March 1940
for G.O. and E.M.

For this time when the dead only are remembered,
And the weight of the blood breaks through the skies,
And the five continents again are separately numbered,
I offer you the pick of my pockets, my bulls'-eyes
   For all children.

Thus I offer you this poem as any man might offer
A steak to a dog, seeking to solve his own conflict
While seeing its delight, so that although he suffer
Another be happy, and that he, too, for his act
   Receive his reward.

Thus I hold out Christ's hand with the neat round sore,
The butterfly, under the glass, crucified to the cork,
Also the terrible voice and the lank lock of hair,
And the rich comfort of the city's acres of dark;
   Refuse what you wish.

Or if you would rather, I will give you the Thames
From Blackfriars Bridge up to Charing Cross,
Or all the forgotten statues to the neglected names,
A perch on the shot-tower, or the level voice
   Of the B.B.C. announcer,

Or the tasselled plane-trees in the Inner Temple;
O, you can have the Tower as your marriage-bed,
And, if you'd wish it, the Abbey as a cradle,
And Richard the First and Lincoln at the head—
   The guardian angels;

And Piccadilly Circus to be your wedding-ring,
And the register to be signed with Cleopatra's Needle
And the fat pigeons on the trees to be ordered to sing
Grieg, since I rejected Mendelssohn for your bridal
    Bus-ride in the City.

O and now and forever I wish that you two may
Be happy, and I hope that the seven seas of the years
Cannot erode your fortunate shores, and that every day
Will be fresh as a flower, and there will be no tears
    As stains on your history.

Varieties of Hero

for J.S.

While you admired the hero, the suave superman,
Debonair in action and slick on the draw
And wished him shown without a flaw,
I, you said, disliked the great Napoleon
And the man whose fingers sprouted in a gun,
Belittled the hero who knew the polar seas
As I my armchair and its cushioned ease,
And seldom let the cheered favourite win.

Yet, of the real truth your guess went wide,
I sought the man now buried in the legend,
The man like you and me whose long road
Did not go undisturbed towards its end;
Whose fear in battle and unpleasant manner
Were known to few, who hid them for his honour.

Samuel Palmer at Reigate

for **G.G.**

Recollecting his vows against corruption,
The old man sat, too mild for curses,
His old thoughts flowed and there was no eruption.
Perhaps he never had desired the purses
That Richmond found behind the mottled faces,
Glazed by the spotlights in the public places?

Settled in neat gentility, to drag out his years
Where his carefully tended weeds were torn
From the correct garden, the old man shed no tears
For all his past, for Ruth among the heavy corn
And the fine impasto of the blossoms which explode
Like fireworks. He could not go back along the road

Of dreams. At times the forbidden portfolio lay open—
Calvert who had forgotten his early vision
For the respectable fantasy, the boring, thin
Mythology, or Finch who had made no impression
Except on a score of half-starved mangy cats:
The Ancients who, lacking the excuse of traditional rats,

Had forsaken the memory of the Interpreter, Blake,
Whose cuts for Virgil still had power to stir
The old man from his lethargy to denounce the fake
That sometimes he approached. Sticky as any burr
These thoughts still clung and he could not forget
Shoreham, the orchards and the hops, a tangled net.

[43]

But there was no doubt the desired spark had gone;
There were too many troubles, his hard wife—
Daughter of Linnell whose round clouds had shone
Above the Claude landscapes of his early life—
The need of money and the nagging itch for fame
Had permanently dimmed the once bright flame.

Palinurus

for C.C.

Lost in the impossible land of exile's return
His dreams are submarine, the warm sea's floor
Has richer forests than he ever knew before,
A thousand hands hold Death at every turn:
Time lingers lovingly about the soft-washed bones;
These gentle tides would never rip the flesh apart,
Prawns have his tendons now, lampreys his heart,
And his dead ears can echo to the mistral's moans.

Before his town window here the tree-tops wave
Like sea-plants through a plate-glass wall;
'Perhaps,' they signal, 'the path across the grave
Leads to the life that's never known to pall?'
In his slack hands the pilot holds the wheel,
The sky grows dark and reefs scrape at the keel.

Six Winters

Six winters since, I dandled on my knee
The neat-tholed toy that was my son,
That yet was more than toy and more to me
Than all the Herodian innocents rolled in one,
Or that child whose mother fled by the Egyptian sea.

Now I am gallows where no mandrake grows,
No bryony twines up my splintering grey shaft;
Though hanging history creaks as the gale blows,
My sole possessions are the leaves that drift
This sodden autumn, waiting cementing snows:

Or else my fancy says I am explorer still,
Haunting the fringes of a never travelled land,
The hypochondriac dreamer, torn by an untrue ill,
Who dares not drop the guide-book from his hand,
Nor venture more than eye's length from the closest hill.

For these six winters of a war which stole
This that I loved so much, have also taken
Much that my time thought good, thought real,
Been X-ray showing the diagnostic much mistaken,
Disclosed the gentle hand grown horned and cruel.

It Was Easier

Now over the map that took ten million years
Of rain and sun to crust like boiler-slag,
The lines of fighting men progress like caterpillars,
Impersonally looping between the leaf and twig.

One half the map is shaded as if by night
Or an eclipse. It is difficult from far away
To understand that a man's booted feet
May grow blistered marching there, or a boy

Die from a bullet. It is difficult to plant
That map with olives, oranges or grapes,
Or to see men alive at any given point,
To see dust-powdered faces or cracked lips.

It is easier to avoid all thought of it
And shelter in the elegant bower of legend,
To dine in dreams with kings, to float
Down the imaginary river, crowds on each hand

Cheering each mention of my favoured name.
It is easier to collect anecdotes, the tall tales
That travellers, some centuries ago, brought home,
Or wisecracks and the drolleries of fools;

It is easier to sail paper-boats on lily-ponds,
To plunge like a gannet in the sheltered sea,
To go walking or to chatter with my friends
Or to discuss the rare edition over tea,

Than to travel in the mind to that place
Where the map becomes reality, where cracks
Are gullies, a bullet more than half-an-inch
Of small newsprint and the shaped grey rocks

Are no longer the property of wandering painters,
A pleasant watercolour for an academic wall,
But cover for the stoat-eyed snipers
Whose aim is fast and seldom known to fail.

It is easier . . . but no, the map has grown
And now blocks out the legends, the sweet dreams
And the chatter. The map has come alive. I hear the moan
Of the black planes and see their pendant bombs.

I can no longer hide in fancy: they'll hunt me out.
That map has mountains and these men have blood:
'Time has an answer!' cries my familiar ghost,
Stirred by explosives from his feather bed.

Time may have answers but the map is here.
Now is the future that I never wished to see.
I was quite happy dreaming and had no fear:
But now, from the map, a gun is aimed at me.

Address to Human Grandeur

How contemptible a thing was human grandeur, which could be mimicked by such diminutive insects as I.—Swift

I

Not less than Death am I the spectator of the crazy pageant
   of history;
The agate eye to see tomorrow tremble like a salt tear on
   the long lash
Of the coast, the ear to hear the voice crying calamity in a
   cruel time.
Not less than the monster Macaulay have I tracked time
   across my teacup,
Than the dwarf Gibbon unpeeled the layered onion of my
   Roman world.
I have seen ten thousand years pressing like pistons in the
   tracks of my tomorrows,
And have had my dreams of a dynasty drowned by the tick
   of a clock.
This is my crackerjack circus, my Barnum and Bailey in
   the arena of the past,
These are my performers from that mad maelstrom,
   playing to drown despair
In a welter of wishes. History, like an escalator, slides
   to my feet,
While I, alone, watch and weep for my wandering and
   bewildered world.

This is my tick of time, my vantage point, tributary of my
   tribulation:

Here I see tears trickle to the Tigris as Genghis Khan, the
 terrible archer,
Pours through proud Persia, and know these hours of
 horror when hate
Bursts in the North. Firmly I grip the hemlock hand, five
 pointed starfish
Or pierced palm, to greet the great, who ran before me
 into time.
I have been Emperor of all the Eastern world, the man of
 the morning sun,
And as flesh fell to fustiness have watched my fancy flake away
While my dead and bloodless brain grew like a gangrene,
 expanding to embrace
The twin Americas and Atlantis under the Atlantic; I have
 been Alexander
Sulking in Syria, and have felt my skin shrivel, glove to
 my armature of bone,
When I was prince of Egypt under the embalmer's expert
 finger.

I have been that pigeon of pride, Napoleon Bonaparte,
 neat as a newt,
Under the monolith minarets of Moscow, flame in the
 sand-sharp snow,
And the dead, decorated with medals of flame, crowned me
 king of the cruel.
I was Caesar, far from the seven hills of home, the goose-
 guarded ramparts of Rome,
Noting the Northern Light that led to the drawn dagger.
 I am Daedalus,
Drugged by the tracer stars, who daily falls to the flint-
 foamed Channel.
The moth of my memory crucifies Christ to the cork of my
 mind's museum.

I am the obsessed Ahab shying from the salmon's leap
while Moby Dick,
Victor in all my visions, blows in the neck of the North
Sea bottle.
Following the assassination of the archangels, I pray to
the planets,
The pale moon of midsummer and the perpendicular
pitiless sun.

II

But, for today only, I am myself, the mildly mad, at home
in the house
Haunted by the terror of my time, am not a Blake blinded
by dreams.
Under six feet of space I occupy, and, so far, a quarter of a
century:
Yet I am a world weeping by the Firth of Forth, the
sword is sheathed
In my scabbard body. I am a child crying out against a
cloud.
In the dominion of the dead I lie with Lycidas, O where
love lingers longest,
I am the sweet splintered bone of the bombed baby and the
mourning mother:
The taut thread of the searchlight, the falling flare,
illuminate my heart,
Caged in cartilage, wrapped in my ribs, dovecote of
destiny, of homing tomorrows.
The astrologer's falsehood falls in the face of my fury and
my tumbling tears
Extinguish the embers of emperors, drown the dreams of
dictators.

O I have been God in my own mind, and saints martyred
by many monarchs:

I have marched by the insatiable Indus and staggered
across the steppes,
Built the Great Wall of China, and commanded history to
commence with me.
O is the blood of children the bread of tomorrow, will the
weeping of women
Water the withered world? Can I place the Plough to
point out the Pole,
Or build with broken bricks a crucible, kiln, to temper this
tormented time?
What will arise from the fumes of the phoenix? Is there a
future fat with promise
Or the prolonged present, an elastic eternity? O could I
pluck the fruit
Of the future, would my heart burst with its bounty or
crumble to cinder?
Now from their stone shelters stare the empty eyes of the
glorious dead
And each is king for the space of his grave, and we weep
for our wandered, our wondering world.

The Butterfly Boy
for G.B.

The butterfly boy who talks with angels,
Or walks with Wordsworth by the riverside,
Angles among the flotsam of the flowing tide,
Or, entomologist, entraps the morning's spangles.
Love is falcon on his quivering wrist,
Whose eyes are hooded by the night's alarms
Against the terrors of the verbal storms
He holds like Ajax, folded in his fist.

On his shoulder sits the evening star
Whispering haunting words of which the least
Are certainly not these, flung in his ear,
Recalling the long road homeward from the East,
Wherein his body became a world's wide map
And rivers ran his veins like mounting sap.

In September 1939

Walking by Roslin, in the wet grass, after the start of war,
Where the pine-trees are straight and sharp as swords,
Our minds drift on like smoke, unblown by fears,
Among the ripening brambles and the chattering birds,
And even, temporarily, we can avoid the mischief of words.

In a field a bent man, with a bottle of carbolic dip,
Scrapes the maggots from the back of an old ewe
And whistles between his teeth at the huddled sheep;
Here the loudspeaker in the farm seems miles away
And we can almost forget the guns down in the valley.

But there is a tight string over our lives;
Pluck it and you will see the arrow start
On its journey to nowhere; twang it and the bee-hives
Will buzz forever in your head. One will depart
On a journey and will leave no broken heart.

The imperishable gold of tomorrow is tarnished
Already. The dreams of rare butterflies are found
To be nothing but dreams, and the mind furnished
With bric-a-brac is declared to be unsound
By the wise who were prepared for such an end.

At Hawthornden there is bombardment by dragonflies
And the willow-wren warbles like a siren;
But back at the farm the baby, three months old, cries
Without tears or grief, without knowing our pain,
To remind you, my dear, that it's six o'clock again.

It would be simple if one could live in a moment forever,
And not care about the future that, taut as a violin string,
Runs out of sight, or if one could gather together
All the most precious moments, like beads on a string;
However, as that is impossible, I do what I can with my
    tongue

To persuade you that, on the other side of this black wall,
The world we built ourselves is still alive
And that some good may come of all this evil;
And that, although tomorrow in the train I may not believe
Anything I say now, the future is certain to arrive.

Various Places

Now the sun shines spangled over Gloucestershire
Over the warm yellow of the soft stone farms
And I standing on this hill-top think I see far
Yet know that none see Europe half so plain
   As I these counties.

The Worcester sand glares scarlet from the pit
And the small carts carry it to the iron-foundries
Whose tall stacks stand sharp beyond the wheat.
Do the iron-masters see Europe half so plain
   As I these counties?

Who walks these hills and treads the stiff bracken
Or rests on the oak-seat beneath the nineteen trees
To rub his nettle stings with crumbled leaves of docken
Cannot find Europe nor see it half so plain
   As I these counties.

Who would see Europe now must learn to climb,
Higher than these easy hills or even Snowdon's peak:
Who would know Europe now must see the ready bomb
That hangs there like the sudden bursts of black smoke
   Above these counties.

The Explorer

I am an intruder in these regions
Where the snow burns a clear flame;
I am a traveller from temperate zones
Who is to a strange country come.

I did not know of this red valley
Where the moon lies for half the year,
Its silver bowl tended by the osprey.
Being civilized I am full of fear.

I had not heard of the whirlpool
That engulfs the sea in winter-time,
Or of the winds that regularly unroll
The ice as carpet to the earth's frame.

I shall not stay here long, I think,
But having learned a little will return.
That I am either raving mad or drunk
Will be proclaimed by those who scorn

The explorers who stumble on the truth.
It would be better to deny with gentle grace
The rumours that precede me of my finds.
But I know now I cannot hold my peace.

The Usual Story

He went from the harsh tower of words,
Ancestral home of his mad angry god,
Who flung the lightning and laid flat the wood,
Crushing the field-mice and the nestling birds.
He went from the high tower his fathers
Had built for him upon the edge of light;
Thinking things different in the world without
He hoped the cues would come to him from others.

He chose the hard path at the cross-roads,
As younger sons had done for many years,
And aped the men he met, the latest modes,
Until he reached the climax of his fears
And thought he recognized the thorny track;
As well he might. It was the same road back.

Last Man at Judgement

Up the declivity to the bridge I climbed,
Expecting the little tugs to shuttle past
As they had done when first I dreamed
Of this extremity; but no stack or mast

Dipped down to scrape beneath the arch.
I, Crusoe of this world, was all alone,
Lord of my sight, and all my careful search
Found no man in any corner of the town.

Fighting the thermometer and creeping ice,
I went among the slow bergs by Thames-side,
But the bright mirror of my ready eyes
Reflected no signs of life nor ebb of tide.

I could remember little but the loud bombs
Around me, then the long dark days of mist,
And falling snow, and ice that steadily came
Towards me out of the North. All was lost.

The anxious plants still struggled in the park
But there was no bee to mix the sexy pollen:
And I was suddenly aware of my world's wreck,
The last of life, the solitary man.

Recapitulation

To walk in the remembered places
Is to stir memories, to try to catch
The worn past and the rainbow faces
In the short flare of a lighted match.
But these things have long been altered
And recollection has grown as hard

As any lime-dripped image in the caves
Where water turns all flesh to stone;
So that the thin past only lives
In the false emotions, joy and pain.

Walking once more upon the ancient roads
I hope that I may meet my dream
As solid-fleshed as the famous gods
Who owned the moor behind my home.
However, the statue silent in the square
Presents the only known face there.

The First Death of de Chirico

Someone had once designed the lonely city,
A man had lived there, loved its squares,
Whose children's feet had trodden down the stairs,
Someone had even called the monuments 'pretty';
A man had lived there who had heart to pity
The child bowling her hoop along the dark arcade,
A man, indeed, who never was afraid
Of the night's tragic melancholy beauty.

Finally, however, even his nerve gave.
He withdrew into an impossible Grecian past
To escape the haunting of his terrible perspective;
The heroic stallion and broken column came at last
To be his only friends on the neglected shore,
Helped him forget that the dark tower stood forever more.

A Personal Note

Here, in this quiet spot, apart
From the turmoil of Europe,
The flurried engine's noisy start
And the bomb smashing hope;
I sit still and think now of you,
Measuring river's pearl against sea's blue;

Think of the sun's glare
And twisted cactus plant
Against this grey and heavy air
And a mast's indolent slant;
Wish I were where you are, or you here,
To stop these minutes tapping at my ear.

I wait the morning paper—
How many killed in Spain?
Yet now, before the deeper
Knowledge of pain,
I give you the minutes of this hour;
All that I have, so treasure them, my dear.

January Poem

I live by this January wind
That smirrs* and blurs the lens
Of life. I know its unkind
Grip at corners; its hand
Cherishing the tendons,
Teaching the nerves to bend.

Not knowing its touch
On heather and sphagnum,
Not having felt its reach
Making the veins itch,
I did not hear it come
And the blood unlatch.

I know I am of the town
Especially in January
When the acid wind is blown
Against my thighs; I know pain
Seeing the ancient granary
Empty, the Phoenix flown.

* *Smirr* is a Scots word—roughly 'to smear', but more expressive.

The Family Skeleton

The family skeleton was, of course, forbidden
To move at all out of his moth-haunted closet;
For even at parties the old could not forget
He lived upstairs, so well and carefully hidden.
With all this secrecy for over thirty years,
The poor ghost thought himself the devil,
Someone well-known, the source of evil
And the first cause of all the children's fears.

At last, remembering the power that he had been,
He made his only and his last decision
And went downstairs with solemn clank of bone,
Encountering only the children's loud derision.
He fled again, finally, into his stuffy loft,
His proud dreams punctured by the way they laughed.

A Temporary Resurrection

There was a cold wind coming from the east
Scattering the leaves and papers in the gardens,
Weaving memories by ponds, sharpening the ice-crust
And disturbing the heart's etiolate wardens.

And I who had been dead for a very long time
Rose from my sofa on the blanching earth,
Tied my bones with tendons, scattering the worms,
And walked anew the ways that lead to birth.

Impotence was there in the fresh spring winds
And gripped the wiry hairs and the hollow bones,
Held them underground with its clammy hands
Mating the rising body with the cold limestone.

As doubt claws holes in the indelible brain,
Enclosed and ill-protected by the mortifying skull,
The mind gains harmony with the falling rain,
And the eyes' serrated sockets drink their fill.

Is it not Passing Brave . . .?

He that knew the answer knew the loss;
As the candle-end's waxed fingers crept
The silent pain through bones, man slept
Fathoming fantasies among the summer grass.
He would not sleep, who'd answered the equation,
He could not move, salt-pillared by emotion.

The vintages of age his reasoned ransom,
The fine-fingered fellow who knew all
Sucked from sad hands the cup of holy-oil,
Sap from a last supper. His was the name
That measured murmurs did not tell aloud,
His was the worm that burrowed in the shroud.

The locksmith of the underworld, his pretty fellow,
Eased out the latchet from the flickering eye,
To let day run, unhindered by a sun-struck sky.
O he is a saint now whose sweet bones are hallowed,
Dry-pickled in the care-carved altar vault
Along with the dead rye and ancient malt.

He is a god now, who was man in the mad flower,
Whose death was answer to the question.
Death answered him and gave him station
Among the bones that made his bower.
The skull's circle holds his enviable voyage;
His memory is a statue on the pigeon's ledge.

Biography

Early suckled in the fear of death
He grew among the tombstones,
Hearing the legendary click of bones
As the corpse expelled its final breath.

He learned how with surgeon's skill
To probe precisely through the skin,
Finding it tissue only, wafer thin;
He admired the symmetry of the skull;

He inspected with eyes set narrow
The reputed pureness of the skeleton,
Finding it false; the hollow bone
Destroyed by suppuration of marrow;

Played elegant tricks with nerves,
Spoiling the harmony of flesh;
Till Death came, keen to flush
The pheasants in his own preserves.

Legend

Up north, somewhere among the dark sea-caves,
Snatching a living from the battered wrecks,
A prisoner of the grey water and granite rocks,
His school friends say the legendary old man lives;
His eyes, they say, are keen as when he shot
The marauding buzzards plunging on the moor;
The crofters are afraid of him and will not dare
The steep-sided gully or the spread mud-flat.

Exactly why he left them none could tell;
He was an ill man to cross, the old wives said,
And there was mention of a killing on the fell.
But these tales do not disturb him. He is dead
And has been so throughout these rumouring years,
While his legend grew, nourished on their fears.

Sometimes Ghosts

Sometimes I watch the ghosts walking,
Tall shapes that I know to expect now;
Sometimes, after midnight, I hear them working,
Mower and tractor against scythe and plough.

Sometimes I am dead when they visit me
Carrying presents to place upon my bed;
I am the other side of time, in a country
Where the owl talks and the mouse leads.

Sometimes I call a ghost by name,
He will not answer; he does not know my voice.
I meet them, neatly clothed in purple flame;
Sometimes I am afraid of their egg-smooth faces.

Sometimes I know I am a ghost myself
But not one of them, a second-hand spirit
That is no longer useful, is left upon the shelf.
Sometimes I think I am a talking ferret.

About Scotland, & C.

I was my own ghost that walked among the hills,
Strolled easily among the ruined stones of history;
The student of geography, concerned with fells
And screes rather than with the subtle mystery
Of action's causes—the quickly overbalanced rock
Upon the passing victim, the stab in the back.

Why did this burn run that way to the sea,
Digging a cutting through stone, moss and peat,
And so become ingredient of whisky?
Why was this glen the cause of a defeat,
The silver bullet in the young man's lung,
The devil's puppet and hero of a song?

That queen herself was lorded by the weather,
And Knox drew sustenance from poverty,
The sharp east wind, the sickle in the heather.
The reiver was cornered in the sudden sortie
Of armoured men lying hidden in the bracken,
And a royal line was by sea-storm broken.

This way the landscape formed the people,
Controlled their deeds with cairn and gully;
And no pretender or well-favoured noble
Had power like dammed loch or empty valley.
Their history's origins lie in rock and haze
And the hero seems shorter than his winter days.

This my ghost saw from the deserted keep
And the left paper-mill forgotten in the slums,
This he saw south among the soft-fleshed sheep
And north-west where the Atlantic drums.
Then, since he'd made no claim to be apostle,
He left, his trophy a neglected fossil.

Thriller

The tall detective on the landing-stage
Waits the arrival of the master-crook,
Time, smuggling drugs inside a clock;
Our sleuth, famed hero of his age,
Wants credit for the villain's death—
That super-murderer who destroyed
The old squire and the village maid,
And felt no satisfaction and no grief.

Watching the passengers as they descend
His eagle glance would penetrate disguise;
Time, however, does not show his hand—
Came by an early boat to trick those eyes:
The great detective's plans depend
Always upon the element of surprise.

This Lonely Month

This long and lonely month
With memory nagging like a gramophone,
Evenings devoted to darts and too much beer,
The early morning rising,
The battering awkwardly upon the typewriter
And the planting of strange seeds.
This long and lonely month.

This long and lonely month
With the emptiness full of fluff and feathers,
The silent house driving me out to walk
Alone along these Essex lanes,
Or to hoe the persistent weeds,
The nettles and the thistles that push up
Inevitably through the month.

O yes, the yellow rock-rose
Shows its wafer petals, and the scabious
Buttons the roadside, and the strawberry
Ripens, and young apples fall.
Yes, the sad prisoners thin the beet
And the cuckoo presses on the ear,
This long and lonely month. . . .

This long and lonely month
Cannot erase my memories,
My last glance back before that corner
Cut like a razor blade.
Nor can I forget the small shadow
Sliding away along the western sky,
This long and lonely month.

This long and lonely month,
My love, has altered nothing in my heart;
In a far country you, too, are lonely,
And these lines I write you now
Send you my love and tell you that I myself
Have been lonely as a leper,
This long and lonely month.

After a Long Time

Nothing has changed, or will; the mirrored room
Still will not let time break or enter.
Splashed by the sentimental band's impartial spume
Is a small silent world of which we are the centre.

Nostalgia's waves froth round us like a tide
Edging its course among the granite rocks,
And loneliness is washed away, flotsam outside
This world freed from the tyranny of ticking clocks.

That tall and slender bottle cannot hold
More of the truth than her beside me here,
The understood silence cannot bicker or scold
For in this place we have forgotten fear.

O the dictatorship of the clock is broken,
And the jumping ball comes luckily to rest,
Time's croupier hands me the counter or token
To change for happiness of which I never guessed.

Though tomorrow raise up the ghosts of the past,
And time return with its fears and its fever,
The image of her beside me will always last
In the mirrored mind, in the mirrored room, forever.

Tomorrow Will Come Soon

Man, the unfortunate animal, watches the new moon crawl
Across the sky, across evil Europe; and tomorrow's dead
Are still aware of their pasts and are aware of all
The things that made their lives. To look ahead
At nothing is their whole ambition. Remember the
    mornings
Of your happiness; remember yesterday and the child
On the brink of ice, laughing at the solemn warnings;
Remember the first-loved's fingers and the way she smiled;

But do not look at the clock—the bland pale face of fate
Hung on the distempered wall, or hear the cracked bell
Marking the hours. Tomorrow will come soon, too late
For some of those, of whom there will be none to tell
How once Love made him King of the Antipodes
And her Queen of Cockayne, or Princess of the Seas.

An Autobiography

When I was very young my nurse took me
Out of the place with the wicker cake-stand
And away from the lady with the feather-boa
To see the woods behind the timbered house,
To sit down under the yellow pussy willows
And gather moss for dressing wounds.

That was at Hunter's Quay, where one night
The guns spoke often, briefer than thunder,
And the next morning David, my brother,
Returned dirty from the pebbly beach,
His plump face smeared with diesel-oil,
Evidence concerning a vanished submarine.

Later, the lady with the feather-boa
Took me on her knee and told me stories,
Ending with one about herself travelling
For a long time into some far country;
Trains running ceaselessly along the single track
Meant that the journey could have no return.

And this had little meaning, for angels and birds
Were much the same and parrots, too, could speak
Clearly when they wished to boast, and death
Was a grey mouse by the roadside, squashed
By the iron-shod wheel of a hay-cart,
And the road was hard and death a fallen feather.

Then there was Gullane, where the east wind
Knocked against the high brick wall
To beg admission, and the green plums
There were strangely sweet, and the red worms
In the water-butt beside the rose-garden
Spun furiously to wave green slime.

And then to the smoky town, to Edinburgh,
Where in the house in Danube Street the hole
In the floor of the dining-room helped our games,
And mock-father walking to the office fell
And broke his leg, a simple fracture mended
Within a minute by the cardboard stethoscope.

Armistice, with many flags and coloured ribbons
Decorating the pram whenever we went out,
And, like a blunt silver-pencil, the airship
That flew slowly over Saxe-Coburg Square,
Distracting attention from the thick gum
That oozed gradually from the cherry-tree.

Now, perhaps, things are not so simple,
War and the guns and the coloured flags
Mean rather more and death, at least, is
A painting by Brueghel, though still a journey
That only runs one way. And I myself?
I myself am not so purely simple.

On Hampstead Heath

The Heath frozen and the flints fixed in the hard earth
Under the rotten birches with the bark as blue as ice,
The privet and laurel leaves twisted down by the cold
And the hole punched with the ferrule though the pond

Are unlike the things I knew these winters past
When the sphagnum crackled under my tacketty boots
And I found the snipe trapped by their beaks in the ice
Which had caught them unaware and fastened like a gin.

Here the yellow clay as crisp as fired bricks
And the hunched blackbirds under the holly-hedge
Where there are no berries, the scum of half-formed ice
On the narrow stream and gulls at the pot-holes:

There the drowned ewe with wool like rigid wires,
The over-eager tup that needed bleeding and blood
That froze black before the morning, the fingers
Numb after tugging hay from the frosted stacks,

The cow calving unexpectedly on the farthest hill
And the brisk smack of the tenant's expensive gun;
The snares in the long grass under the fences
And the rabbits with the hard collar of fragile fur.

Here the hard paths repeat the footsteps
Like the monotonous voices of idiot boys repeating
The orders they were given, to clean the byre,
Build up the dung-heap by the stable and feed the heifer.

From this hollow, looking up, I watch the tree-tops
Swinging in the gale and feel the sharp flakes
Of the first snow falling against my glasses,
And see the red brick of the garden suburb.

In these two places, I am the constant factor
That can see the difference and compare the likeness:
The one place an island where the clear sea crashed
Up the crescent of sand, spray on a face a mile away,

And the other, this heath, where the walkers
Are always within easy reach of home and the cars
Come noisily along the frozen dividing roads.
I make these places, in my mind, my own.

Excess

'Excess, excess,' cried William Blake,
Loathing the poised and classic stance,
The mealymouther who would take
His satisfaction from the half.

Too much was always for the best,
Restraint was evil and would kill
Those who suffered it. The repressed
Were the unhappy, the crooked and the ill.

Man should live on such a scale
That each emotion was an Albion's whim;
Only the timid would retreat and fail
To reach the peak of their desire.

Loving by halves will soon destroy
Both the lover and the loved;
The sweetness of the words will cloy,
The tepid truth inflict a wound.

So, when I love, let my excess
Stride like a giant towards its fall,
That in the end it may confess
There, at the least, it was not small,

And that its love was no mistake,
That it was right in giving what it had;
That all the words of William Blake
Proved justly that the world was mad.

The Present

Love, should I sleep with Death's own daughter,
You'll know there is no breach of trust,
For as my body rots, with worm or water,
Where I lie, I'll sleep, forgetting lust.
Someday, of course—I can't say 'No'—
We'll both be dead, and I can only hope
You'll find Death a decent chap to know,
One with whose whimsies you can always cope.

Well, you and I won't give a tinker's damn
For we'll be past all faithlessness and fears.
Knowing what was true from what was sham
We'll let Death and his daughter wag their ears,
Do all their parlour tricks and laugh and shout:
What we are now is what I care about.

Autumn Campion

Curiously, considering the nearness of the frost,
I found a campion, her flower, in bloom
Among the fallen leaves, one flower, half-lost
In summer's shambles in the autumn-silent wood.

This small pink bud above the crumpled brown
Shone clearly and a klaxon-throated jay
Flashed blue and rose before me: stooping down
I touched her flower but left it growing;

And all the wood seemed suddenly as bright
As if spring had come back and I was glad
Her star winked happily in autumn's night
Where, moonlike, I was faithful, and was mad.

Combat Report

I walk at dawn across the hollow hills,
Throwing egg-shells at the little moon.
Explosive for my bombs are puffball spores,
Measured out carefully, with a silver spoon.

Up there the heavy artillery is banked
To resist the bee that booms along the valley;
Machine-gun nests are placed among the crags
In case the eagles dare to make a sally.

Single-seater planes engage the curlew
Circling above the peat-moss and bog-myrtle.
The wound the old tup got an hour ago
Has since, I have to state, proved fatal.

Luckily the blind-worm does good work
And dodges past the enemy's best scout;
He rallies the wethers and attacks their rear,
Turning their predicted victory to a rout.

I walk at evening on the shattered moors,
Placing tea-leaves on the ancient cairns
In memory of the old tup and dead plover.
I walk at midnight on the trampled ferns.

Worm Interviewed

It said it was the resurrection's worm,
Coiling its long whip in the empty vein;
Again, it said, I am the carnal worm
Sprung sweetly from the tissue of the head;
I, and I only, know the marrows of the brain,
The mysterious issue of the infertile egg.

I caused the mind storm in the summer,
Throwing my long spear in the blood;
I caused the cracking of the missing rib,
My teeth the chisel and my eye the hammer.
Being the maggot in the newly dead
I heard the last pulse come bitterly.

I stole the tendon from the fractured foot
As scaffolding to bolster up my nest;
I stole the nerve that held the eye to socket,
Now dropped aimlessly upon the cheek.
I was the asp about the virgin's breast
That made the milk to run at Christmas time.

I was the first thing and am last;
I made the bone that cowered in the womb,
My nest about it made the firm hard limb.
I am the maker who does not count the cost
Of the long shelter of the tomb.
I am the priest who battens on the dead.

Joan Miró

Once there were peasant pots and a dry
  brown hare
Upon the olive table in that magic farm;
Once all the showmen were blown about the fair
And none of them took hurt or any harm;
Once a man set his fighting bull to graze
In the strict paths of the forgotten maze.

This was that man who knew the secret line
And the strange shapes that went
In dreams; his was the bewitched vine
And the crying dog in the sky's tent.

Once he had a country where the sun shone
Through the enchanted trees like lace,
But now it is troubled and happiness is gone
For the bombs fell in that fine place
And the magician found when he had woken
His people dead, his gay pots broken.

Northwards the Islands

Northward the islands and the sullen shore,
The bald rocks where sulk the summer seas;
Distantly, as in a shell held to the ear,
I can remember their petulant noise
Quickening in winter to a sullen roar.

The leisurely seal fishing from the rock
And the otter trapped beside the burn,
The silver sand with network of brown wrack,
Were once my life, but I cannot return
To scythe the corn or build a stack.

The difference has grown in me,
The islands stay the same. No change
Is possible for me, who move so quickly
To strengthen my acquaintance with the strange.
Tomorrow someone else, but 'I' today.

Where I am going and where I will end
Do not concern me for the present.
Nostalgia for the past I have, and find
It is the imminence of the future I resent,
Not my romantic leanings to the land.

Migration

Blown south by autumn winds that drive
To the far shores, I found my short shadow
Vanish as the tall clocks struck twelve
And I sank among the reeds that grew
In swamps below Egypt and the Nile,
Content as any drake upon the alien soil.

My comrade on the journey dashed his head
Against the lightship anchored in the channel,
But I, of old, was wise and paid no heed
To these attractions; plumes from a funnel
Were my guide across the storm-streaked sky,
Were my sole passport to the sheltered bay.

Yet now, in Spring, I wish I could accept
The offers held by papers from the north
That tell me of the weather and are adept
In description of the country of my birth.
Sickening of sun and papyrus and cranes
I remember the thin-drawn wedge of swans.

Soon I will leave the heat-baked plain
And the mirage dancing in the haze;
Hearing my wave length called again
I count on my fingers the number of days
Since I lost my shadow. Time to return
I find, clung like a gull to a liner's stern.

Do You Believe in Geography?

No one now can understand that chart;
The crossed lines that might have stood for gold
Were found to stand for death, the clockwork heart
Failed during exercise, too used to leisure,
And the dug hole was quickly silted up.

It is a long time since the last hermit died
And the last ornithologist walked the marshes
Tracing the rare avocet that always cried
Just ahead until the collector shot it down
Where the stranger bittern sometimes boomed.

These, they say, had known the secret track
Across the fens, between the tall osiers
And the cotton grass and the thick black
Mud that sucked the slipped or reckless foot
And took the testing pebble out of sight.

But these all died before the map was found,
Before the word lay richly in men's mouths,
Leaving no hints; it was their native ground,
The paths for them required no detailed plans.
So no one now can understand that chart.

In September 1937

Coming, in September, through the thin streets,
I thought back to another year I knew,
Autumn, lifting potatoes and stacking peats
On Mull, while the Atlantic's murky blue
Swung sluggishly in past Jura, and the hills
Were brown lions, crouched to meet the autumn gales.

In the hard rain and the rip of thunder,
I remembered the haze coming in from the sea
And the clatter of Gaelic voices by the breakwater,
Or in the fields as the reapers took their tea;
I remembered the cast foal lying where it died,
Which we buried, one evening, above high-tide;

And the three rams that smashed the fank-gate,
Running loose for five days on the moor
Before we could catch them—far too late
To prevent an early lambing the next year.
But these seemed out of place beside the chip-shop
And the cockney voices grumbling in the pub.

In September, I saw the drab newsposters
Telling of wars, in Spain and in the East,
And wished I'd stayed on Mull, their gestures
Frightened me and made me feel the unwanted guest,
The burden on the house who having taken salt
Could never be ejected, however grave his fault.

In September, we lit the fire and talked together,
Discussing the trivialities of a spent day
And what we would eat. I forgot the weather
And the dull streets and the sun on Islay,
And all my fear. I lost my count
Of the ticks to death, and was content.

Easter in Essex

This is the season of dyed eggs and woolly chicks,
The time of packed knapsacks and of excursions,
Of the affectionate couples in the crowded flicks;
And I spend it in this land that's spread so flat
It asks the sea to roll over it, over the cowslips,
The ancient rights of way and the chestnut buds.

Walking beside a sprouting field I watch
The cock-pheasant strut with ringed neck straight,
Proud in security, safe till the eggs hatch
And till the keeper's darlings learn to fly;
But the abrupt shot at hawk or hoodie-crow
Still sends it rocketing towards the trees.

There is sixpence admission to the windmill,
Although a strong gale blew two sails away,
For it appeared recently in a popular film;
In the forge the blacksmith spends his time
Making an ornamental gate or a fire-iron stand
For the cattle graze on the once arable fields;

The ice-cream merchant stops his gaudy van
Beside the common, and with penny clenched
In hot hand the eager village children run
To catch him. Small boys with stones have broken
The windows of the house with the sign painted,
In crude letters, 'Beware this house is haunted.'

The beech-logs hiss and crackle in the open fire
And the oil light is kind to the urban eyes
Dazzled so long by the arc-lamp and neon's glare.
On the white walls hang pot-lids and blue plates
And glass pictures—the noble marquis, the fond meeting,
And the formal red-clad man engaged in partridge-
  shooting.

Wandering in the woods again among bee-orchids,
Mauve anemones and the jacks-in-the-pulpit,
I find a solitary oxlip and in my progress
Forget Hitler in Austria and the arranged ballot;
The snap of a branch beneath my ambling feet
Sounds only what it is, no distant pistol shot;

And lying at night in the oak-timbered room
I am glad of the familiar arms about my body
And the loved voice whispering my name.
Half-sleeping I see the headlights cross the ceiling,
And waking hear birds moving in the thatch
And the flowered curtains flapping on the sill.

As the stagnant water moves in the duck-pond
When a frog pushes up for air among the weeds
So, anxiously, moves the thing I call my mind
Over the countryside, trying to forget the road
That leads me back to town, beyond the last tent
Of the fortunate hiker and his sunburnt girl.

During an Air-Raid

I

On the south side of the city, sheltered from space,
And from the quavering and menacing sirens,
I let my mind wander, a kestrel to capture
The survivors of this holocaust of my Siberian hopes.

O and my mind is a man, more mammoth
Than the shrapnel, Junkers and searchlights;
Taller than Everest, I totter while a star
Nestles upon my shoulder, a planet my parrot.

II

Alone with this ghost of myself, my body's peak
In the Pleiades, my limbs longer than Asia,
And the sun in my loins, I look at this lovely land
And the places that are precious with people.

Cherishing Lambeth not for its priests and its bishops,
But for Blake who saw Jerusalem pillared
In Golder's Green and on Primrose Hill, who, O declare it,
Discovered the word *golden* in eighteen ten:

Highgate for Coleridge and the drugged deep sleep;
And Hampstead for many, not least for Constable
Who looked at the wind and the trees, and for Keats
Whose lung lay later by the Bay of Naples;

For Linnell, the patriarch painter, and his son-in-law,
Palmer, the lonely heart in the hand of money,
And for a dozen others who saw the pike
Pout in the ponds and the sand slake in the pits.

Omit Stratford, that centre of sentiment, but discover
Southwark where Chaucer counted his company,
And Rydal Mount in the autumn when the daffodils
All are dead and the wind whips upon Windermere:

Let my body's ghost, birn in a ghastly dream,
Cover them up, keep them safe from the deadly Dornier,
And the magnesium-bomb with its pale primrose flare.
Let me nurse Norwich as a courtesy to Cotman,

And my body arc like a bow across Salisbury.
I am brother to the Long Man lying at Cerne Abbas,
And sleep with Fingal in the filigree cave on Staffa.
I was the archer assaulted Yorkshire with stone arrows

And shot from the sky at the butt of Stonehenge.
Let these things live in the light to delight,
And these purr their promises to those who come after
The daylight raid, the roars and the crashing of crowns;

After the conflagration of corn in the stacks,
The fracture of fliers by the Icarus-gorged sun,
And the destruction of tombs by inquisitive bombs,
Death drains from the heights of heaven on the weeping
    fields.

III

Now I am alone in the womb of a new world,
Listening to the crunch and stammer of guns,
A grain of grit loose in a giant gourd,
A man swung in the lonely lap of death;

And neither bird nor branch can beckon
Me out of my jungle of feathery fear
That dusts my face with the taint of destruction.
This slaughter of stone is the slaughter of steel.

O this earth, I say to the wrecked world, is ample for all,
As rich as a ripe rowan with bunches of berries;
Yet night is broken with light, with bursting bombs,
And houses that once were happy are tumbled tombs.

Valleys are velvet beneath my sleeping head,
And trees are tender as fingers drying my tears.
Dawn may display to the world the folly of fury
And the waves of weeping break on a shattered city.

The Darkling Plain

The economic grammar of a brutal time
Rivets its chains, shackling more souls
Than Greece in glory did. Beneath the scrolls
Of Roman law, corrosive as unslaked lime,
The vanquished melt away. Still the voices
Are strident. The children can forget
That love, while loving, also can regret
The peaks it climbed, that the heart rejoices

But is wounded; that, on the empty plain
Of sleepless nights, all courage can retreat,
And dark despair be worse than any pain;
That hell is also here, upon an East Side street.
A hermit, suffering all its wrongs alone,
The heart remains within its bower of bone.

Note on Modern Witchcraft

Secured in his bloated face and trivial mouth:
'I sold my lord for silver, sir,' he said,
'Thinking him subversive, by his dreams misled.
I used him, sir, as nourishment in drouth.'
This seemed excuse enough and we forgave
The hungry rogue who shortly cut his throat
To prove he still had blood—the passing stoat
That sickened was already earmarked for the grave.

'Sir, in my day,' said Time, drivelling no doubt,
'Those who were friends remained as such,
But days have changed—the turncoat cringing lout
Is God.' He stumbled awkwardly upon his crutch.
Poor Time. He'd grown so old and out of date,
He did not know it was our friends we'd hate.

A Garland for Mr Eliot

Strictly contrived, the principles declare
That death is not averse to pleasantry;
The green mummy turned to gold must share
A small portion of the Inferno's immortality:

Also observed, the country village where
The good men flourished in their solitude—
'Good' meaning more than canticle or prayer;
Further, the soldiers marcelled in parade

Provided excuse for poetry: words would share
The late drinkers shambling from the pub,
And Tiresias' unexpectant eye upon the stair,
Goldenrod, New England's rocks, or scuttling crab.

The curious obsessions formed the mind, aware
Of the sad ways men made toward their aim,
Even the gestures his hero could not dare
Became the impulse which created him.

The Anticlimax

Melville, rolled round in bladder-wrack,
Dreamed of the terror of the great white whale,
Though in his later years the tide was slack,
No breeze gave promise of a bellying sail.

Blake, when the vision was magnesium clear,
Saw man break through his hindering flesh
To grasp eternity, but himself knew fear
Trapped in his own time's economic mesh.

Swift, whose indignation knew no bounds,
Had curious prescriptions for a people's ill,
But crazed, in a tower, paced out his rounds,
Uncertain of the truths his words would spill.

Pope found his age diseased, carbuncular,
And taught his pen to slash out and deride,
But Lady Mary saw him as he was, homuncular,
And flowering bitterness was grafted on his pride.

We, in our turn, start out upon the race,
Filled with ambitions which we will soon achieve,
But find, on taking breath, that every place
Is where we were when first we said we'd leave.

A Child in the Middle Forties

After long wars and passages of disaster,
Hearsay of deaths on far-off horrible islands
And under the hills of Europe, the master-
Key turns in the lock; she only understands

That she was little and far too young
To plouter in puddles where once bombs fell,
Or to go out and about, to wander among
The people who trimmed the edges of hell.

And now in a blue and party dress,
She does not think of things to come,
The world of tomorrow can never distress
Her estate as small as the nail of her thumb,

Where everything works the way it should,
And the devil is only noisy in church;
The pure mind knows of nothing but good
And the rest can go hang, or lie in the lurch,

For her laughter would make of any complaint
Something untruthful, smelling of treason,
Something disgusting and nastily quaint—
Right out of place in the holiday season.

The Foundation of the Royal Society 1660

Mountains of prejudice and ignorance surrounding
Their enquiries had to be climbed or levelled down
So that the real world of wonders could, perhaps,
Be reached, explored in detail and the truth shown
To be greater and more remarkable than all the lies.
God's Wisdom in Creation was not easily known.

Then there were the opponents, who adhered
Leech-like to the fleshy body of the old school;
What had been made was not for man to question.
It was simple to dismiss the enquirer as a fool,
A crazy, blasphemous, dangerous and evil babbler
Whose victorious arguments made him the devil's tool.

Of course, it could not come at once, the shelves
Sagged with the dusty pamphlets, creaked with lies
And dreams. Boyle, for example, hoped that gold
Might be the alchemist's reward, his prize
For the experiments with air, with flame and frost,
The small success among a million hopeless tries.

As the old men died off, it became quite clear
That truth was glorious and destined to prevail;
God's Wisdom was explained; He'd given man
The pursuit of knowledge for an holy grail.
In this new world, with everything to find,
There were no whispers of an ultimate betrayal.

Rivers : On Living in Brooklyn

Lifting its fuss of tugs, its floating trains,
The East River runs by Brooklyn, above
The tunnels, and where the shadow stains
Of the bridges shiver as the waters move

Slowly toward the statue and the sea.
The question that remains, is whether
This side or the other matters to me
And if rivers are worth all the bother

They have caused : it would seem that
One side always had to be home.
In London, where the Thames' flat
Grey waters split the city the same

As here, I always tried to live
On the North; and yet you might say
The South had as much to give—
More, considering the light of day.

On the Seine, too, it was the left bank
Which I chose, despite the fact
That there was room on the right to think,
To move freely and to act.

And now, from this island, to go
Ten minutes journey under the East
River seems as though
I was travelling into my past

When I was born by the River Forth
And lived on the South side,
Looking always up to the North
Over its sometimes blue wide

Expanse. There can be no reason
To consider a passage across water
A special deadly kind of treason,
But, all the same, I falter,

And the East River carries its load
Over the tunnel where I now ride,
Watching the black walls slide
Back, my forward move so easily betrayed.

William Cowper's Hares

Lepus europaeus were the poet Cowper's pets,
The common hare, long-legged and long of ear;
Received, after his third affliction, to bring cheer:
He nourished three, of several proffered leverets.
Of rabbits, *Oryctolagus cuniculus,* he had five:
These were not favoured like the darling hares
Who heard the Olney Hymns and muttered prayers
With which the poet sought to keep himself alive.

Tiney had sullenness that was a cause for mirth,
Bess was bold but died too young for praise;
Puss was the sweet who shared the poet's hearth
Twelve years—lacking but thirty little days.
Three chase bachelors enjoyed the poet's chat
While the unchristened rabbits in the stable sat.

Love Poem for the New Year 1952

Ready again to take the usual route—
So long familiar—through the bitter seas
Of winter, vaguely he wondered if astute
Steering would carry him through these

Floes and shuddering, calving bergs,
Which had already smashed the armoured prow
Of every craft he'd ventured on the voyage.
Ahead, the Aurora Borealis' challenging glow

Promised him nothing but fidgeting discontent—
The seas of winter were already near—
The ship yawed with the clumsiness of misspent
Skill—charts smudged with the ashes of a year.

His unprotesting hand lay on the helm,
Resigned again to the inevitable trip
Across the winter's shifting, snarling realm.
Then, suddenly, he was conscious that the ship

Had altered course, that the stars swung
Round, while charts flipped wildly before
His startled eyes—birds impossibly sang
And it was not winter ahead any more.

In a little time he felt her hand
Beside his own upon the twirling wheel.
Over her shoulder, as he turned, the land
Shone brightly, already he could feel

The tingle of the sun upon his cheek.
Hand firmly placed on hers, he set course
South once again, overjoyed to break
So easily through cold oceans of remorse.

Broken Arrowheads at Chilmark, Martha's Vineyard

Glint of white quartz on the pale cream sand,
Or sparkle of worked stone, red, black or green;
The eye, unwillingly trapped, impels the hand
To weigh these fragments of what once had been.

Here then there sat the knapper of the flint,
With fire and careful tap he shaped the head;
From this dark pit he drew stone without stint,
Stones for his working. But he has been dead

A long time. The nickel case of the twenty-two
Corrodes in the salt air. The Indian on relief,
Or plumbing, is hardly the same Indian who
Discarded his failures without petulance or grief.

Perhaps the working of quartz was waste of time;
But such waste and inefficiency could contrive
Lastingness—the paper shell-case molders into grime.
These sharp and many coloured chips survive

While rain and storms erode and centuries elide.
Efficiency seems trivial and our artifacts must pass
As impermanent symbols that cannot lie beside
The arrowhead in the clump of blue-eyed grass.

A Mantelpiece of Shells

The crimp and whorl of conch,
Serrated slot of cowries, stropped
Edge of razors, cup of nautilus,
Fan of the scallop, the sundial's
Coiled watch spring and the scrolled
Edge of the olives. The sound of surf
In the gastropod cupped to the ear.

But more than this. The memory
Recalls the short turf by the Scottish shores;
The anvil of the thrush, where Helix,
Sparsely nourished on the dune bents,
Was broken; the New England roads
Where, bomberwise, the hungry gull
Exploded the quahog; the seed scallop

Thicker than sand along the shores
After the storm; the flushed cowries
Of the Firth of Clyde and the rough coast
Of Northumberland; and jingle shells,
Tangerine, peach, and lemon, sparkling
The beach at Vineyard Haven; and vines
Festooned plumply with *escargots*.

Then, too, the truck on Eighth Street
Crammed with conchs—suffused
Pinks, purples, and browns peddled
For a quarter—stripped of the green moss
That covered those from Menemsha Pond;

Cockles by silver sand on Barra;
Black whelks from a stall in a London street;

Piddocks and angel's wings, borers;
And barnacles on driftwood—acorns
Of legendary geese. The disarray
Of an oyster against the precise flare
The scallop with the turquoise eyes presents;
The limpet's gyre, and the slipper's shelf.
These are the shells that I have known.

But that pink murex on the mantelshelf,
From Florida via Chicago's Shedd,
Japanese treasures from MacArthur's,
Cuban land snails from Central Park West,
Hold out their promises of places
Still to see, of seas to hear, and order
To observe. The spiral towers

Still hide the great adventure:
The Sargasso of the mind welcomes
Such symmetry among its tangled wrack.
Listen once more, to shell from near or far:
The surf still rolls these empty houses
Over the shingle and the sand,
Still breaks them on the granite rocks,

And still the sight and sound recall
Places known and places still to know.
The mind hankers for the angel's wings
And borer's skill, to learn the architecture
That can make so much perfection
From a little lime and silicate.
Listen, the ebbing tide has turned:

These dead, still shells are whispering
Of summer. In the museum cases,
Muted by glass for the moment, lies the roar
Of all the surf that beats up beaches
Round the world; the Aegean lies
In this that made the Tyrian purple.
Here are the more than seven seas

And more than seventy thousand sounds
Distinguishing the shores where, cast
By storm, discarded by the tide
The makers of the shells wither and vanish,
Leaving the shells themselves to bleach,
To powder down again, to be absorbed
Into the vast spiral that will throw up others.

A Narrow Sanctuary

In narrowness love lies—and sometimes lies—
Truth strays or staggers in our narrow ways:
Still, through the narrow truth of thighs,
We find the neatest boundary of our days.

Through the narrow alley of her thighs,
Come truths that might the ordered stars amaze,
So that her slender outlines daze
Those who insist that lying talks of lies.

The narrow confine of her body says
Such things of love, shows vistas that surprise
Those who know vision only through the eyes
Or hold the tongue alone lavish in its praise.

And, in this narrowness, mirages rise,
Distances open under endless skies,
In which love lives and nothing ever dies;
Truth here is naked, seeks for no disguise;

Her arms hold truths no enemy can seize:
Love's narrow truths are wider truths than these
Found in dark solitudes by those called wise
Who did not know the narrowness, the prize.

Strayed in her loins gentleness now lies,
Learned of truths that time cannot suppress
Which, daily like our sun, will still arise
Till love itself lies closed in narrowness.

Max Ernst

The nightingale frightened the children where
Loplop lived by the edge of the lake,
The way to Paradise lay through the core
Of the apple chewed by the famous snake,

And those who got there found that Hell
Had turned the creatures into plants,
That where Max walked the trees would spill
Trailing tendrils made of ants.

The owl had roots and could not fly,
The creepers chased the static lion,
And the stone king wept beside the quay
Because he'd eaten his way to Zion

And found its taste like simple bread
While it looked like cake or an aubergine,
And nothing was as it seemed—instead
Of his new-found love an ageing queen.

Alexander Calder

When one leaf, left hanging on a bough
Pruned sharply by the quickness of the frost,
Fluttering, turns sideways and is lost,
The watcher's eye is opened and sees, now
One shape becoming many as it moves.
In arranged patterns the slow planets turn
But do not alter, so that the eye can learn
Movement controlled in unseen grooves.

Here leaf and planet can combine
To shift upon their slender wires,
Can circle, searching for a line
Or soar around sharp metal spires.

These captive stars are docile and obey
Their maker's whims of change and interplay.

Jacques Lipchitz

Always the sacrifice, the loud-lunged rooster
Boasts for a moment of his once important act,
And is not conscious of the Achillean defect
Which makes him prey of the ceremonial wrestler:
Caught for a moment in the ultimate hold,
With slash of spur against an ungreaved shin,
The sacrifice protests the betrayal was the sin
Of man as strong as this, as firmly tholed
As him who with a slowly tightening grasp
Reduces the proud crowing to an expiring gasp.

Yves Tanguy

The slender dignity of isolated bones
Who are gregarious in a lonely place
Where wires sing as sharp wind whines
Among the melting monuments of ice;

The arctic sun shines over all
And snow or sand are tinted where
The sun's hard rays begin to fail,
Where magic sources start to pour

A fluid spectroscope across the scene
In which these actors hesitate,
Who are not human but remain
Emblems of all which can be met

In those who seek in moving hordes
Assurance that loneliness does not exist,
And that continual contact, flowing words,
Will form an easy substitute for trust.

These lonely beings could be ourselves,
Living in crowds, who are afraid
To risk more than carefully cut halves—
Ourselves, eternally living, always dead.

The Drawings for Guernica

for Pablo Picasso

The woman weeps forever as if her tears
Would wash away the blood and broken limbs,
And the tortured horse whinnies and climbs
Iron hoof on broken beam towards electric stars.
Hands hold withered flowers, the broken sword
And the great arm reaches out with a lamp.
The frightened child in its mother's clasp is limp,
Too terrified to listen to the comfortable word.

Still the great bull stands inside the shattered room,
Inside the world, and still the crouching woman runs
Feeling the child moving in her tightened womb,
Thinking of the small features and the forming bones.
Shut in forever by the grey wall the woman weeps
While the mad horse plunges up the useless slopes.

Paul Klee

The small man suffers the indignities of childhood,
And is made to walk under ladders and caught
By the blind of darkness in the cat-tormented night.
He is terrified by mice and sickened by blood;
Wolf-fanged horses chase after him along the road
And the tight-rope that he walks will always sag
When he has reached the centre so that his soft leg
Is pierced by the pine-needles of the magic wood.

And yet, in the middle of the formal garden,
He finds time to play at noughts and crosses,
And he is master of the sharp wasp whose burden
Of pollen fertilizes the tall elaborate grasses.
In the enchanted ponds are luminous fishes
And paper-boats with cargoes of his wishes.

Henry Moore

A tree grows and rocks have weight;
Arms are the branches and the dark caves
Are what you care to call them, history's graves,
Sex, or the womb, or even man's estate
When, hidden in his own tunnels, he lay
Waiting for the morning, the siren's clear
Note postponing the surging of his fear
Through the long emptiness of appalling day,

Till once again he would be landscape,
Hills and the hollow rocks his urgent form
Designed to stand the crashing of the storm
That could not injure him or change his shape,
These immemorable curves which gentle rain,
Sun, and the cracking ice had smoothed,
To make of him the still unaltering part
Of the slow scenery in the sculptor's heart.

André Masson

Here fish and insects fight,
Carnivorous horses grapple,
Plants flower in the night,
A shape devours an apple;

Birds plunge from the air,
The tiger masks its grins,
The centaur prances where
Death's domain begins.

The subtle line is master
Of this kingdom now,
Explores each fresh disaster
With the casualness of a plough,

Turns up the broken shards,
These mosaics of a crime,
The fortune-teller's cards
And turtle, young in time;

The gliding birds are snared
In the voracious eyes;
The skeleton stands bared
Inviting the unwise

To step in death's dominions
With a ballet-dancer's poise,
Or faltering on dead bird's pinions
Perch on the fabled joys,

These fabled trees of bliss
Where queens and meteors kiss.

The Grave of Washington Allston, Cambridge, Mass.

Abstracted from the snow the stone block
Stands out; only his name and the two dates
Upon it can attract the eyes of those who pass
Hurriedly, their minds full of the fall of states,
The professor's nod, or punctuality for class.
What does the name mean in the trimmed rock?

Forgotten now is the enormous nightmare,
The nearly completed work that, all the time
For over twenty years, crept back toward the bare
Canvas, forgotten too the epic and the rhyme,
The man who once stood with Coleridge where
The Roman stone sparkled in the sun's sharp glare.

Martin, borrowing the theme, had great success;
Belshazzar's Feast astonished all the town
To make the artist famous, but, by then,
The American painter had returned to settle down
To paint and unpaint, to wonder when
Luck would think him ready or fit to bless.

Like the emptiness the obsession grew:
God would not let him die until the end
Had been reached. Only a selected few
Were allowed to see the wreckage; each, a friend,
Hesitated to say what all the time he knew—
That this desperation could make nothing good or new.

The artisan, entering to repair the wall,
Could not turn face to look upon the paint,
Or see the nearly twenty thousand lines the advice
Of Gilbert Stuart had made, these faint
Curves and rulings in white chalk, the price
Of that perfection he wished for above all.

So the plain stone tells nothing of his history,
And the passengers in the orange buses are unconcerned
With this name which stands above the snow,
Or with the nearly finished picture which returned
From England, to suffer the long and slow
Destruction of these years of mystery.

Northern New Jersey:
Near Warwick, N.Y.

Beyond the dark red barns, lined white
Around the windows and the doors,
The mist lies on the hilltops, light
As a hackle drifting here or there.

Closer to hand, the chickens stutter,
And above the clouds the crows collect
With harsh cawing; quietly the mutter
Of crickets in the walnut trees intrudes.

Under the enormous apple, worm-infested,
The blue of chicory sprinkles the grass
Down to the old ditch where, unmolested,
The painted-turtles crawl in the tangle.

The milkweed's curious pods expand,
And a vast heron levers lazy wings;
Tassels hang from stalks which stand
In military rows to reach the farm.

The soil of rich profusion shows
Its flowers and fruits impartially;
Through Tranquillity the traveller goes,
Or drives past little Amity to shop.

Upon this Rock
for H.P.

By pain of stone and wearing down of bronze,
By plaster scrambled with excelsior,
Things come out which were not things before,
And bodies letch with all the grace of swans;

So thus, the strong wings that Leda knew
Holding her steady, while the beak applied its kiss
And she experienced that unsuspected bliss,
Show how they became one symbol—never two;

And the twin-backed beast is common here,
The single symbol seems to search
For another one on which to perch
To make its abundant motives clear:

In excellent amity these forms combine
Whose easy couplings show that sex
Should not be feared, and should not vex
The wife, the harlot or the concubine.

Here Leda and the Centaurs speak
Of love and parentage unknown
To those whose lechery was thrown
At such who did not understand, those weak

Longings petered out, who lived alone
And did not like it. Teach them, O plaster,
Bronze, that their disaster
Lay in their fear of attitudes of stone.

Bronxville

Restrained colonial brick and acorns on the ground,
And the girls in wash-bleached jeans with books
Under their arms, and the poet stretched on the grass
Talking about Yeats and the love-affair with the wound
Of the expected preliminaries that never came to pass,
While there is just a suggestion of sex under the oaks.

This one, tip-tilted breasts under a yellow blouse,
Disapproves, morally, of Eliot and his church,
And that one thinks that to make poems is nice
But spends her time in resentment and grousing
About her lack of interest in technique, the price
She'd get as reward would not justify the research.

This one is simple and desires to know how Yeats
Compounded his odd philosophy to suit his peculiar self,
A clandestine marriage of Madame Blavatsky with Blake
And a solemn yogi attending the nuptials and the mating;
Behind, all the time, was the middle-aged man's aching
Knowledge of how long the burning desire had been
    shelved.

And so they slip through the fingers, like fish in a tank,
Freed, or so it is hoped, from bias and mean restraint,
Able to accept the world as it is to them, or to try
To make it a little better, and not to expect the thanks
Of those whose long fate it has been to abide
In the shadow of loneliness in the acres of want.

Onomatopoeic Ornithology

The little voices of these birds declare
Their names aloud, precise and clear,
Sharp notes glinting in the brilliant air:

Amazed, the listener can stand and hear
Identity announced in call or whistle,
As when the pacific plover cries 'Killdeer',

Beside its nest by charlock or thistle.
In alfalfa he may chance to see
A so-called sparrow insist it is Dicksissel,

While, hunting on a twig, the Chickadee,
Boasting with all its might,
Would steal the cognomen of declared Phoebe

Who'd never dare to Chuck-will's-widow's mite
To the plaid-clad gleaner who'd think
In Anglo-Saxon terms, proclaim himself Bob-white.

The Towhee that takes on the name Chewink
Soon brags its whole disguise away.
Only the human ear would seek the link
To join identity to what birds say.

The Louse

Robert Hooke, 'Micrographia', 1665

This is a creature of extreme impertinence
Who tramples heedless on the quality;
A saucy beast without the shadow of pretence,
He sucks our blood from mere frivolity.

The public head that wears a crown
Cannot be reached for easy scratching,
So preference for such is shown
Where eggs lie safe until their hatching.

Beneath the microscopic light
His fringed bulb-eyes look back;
Perhaps he's short of good foresight
But does not suffer from the lack.

Observe the plate, engraved with care,
With louse displayed as large as cat,
Bristled with elephantine hair,
His smugness increased with his fat.

Grown to the largeness of a lion, the mole
Would range around like Genghis Khan:*
The systems of the louse, *systole* and *diastole*,
Would make an empty shell of every man.

* For the mole see Rev. J. G. Wood, *Homes without Hands*, 1865, p. 15.

The polished lens made man less sure
That he was chosen of the universe;
Until that time he'd felt secure
But suddenly God's humour seemed perverse—

Perfection wasted on a parasite!
The grave preachers trembled in their thought,
But cheered, all would come right
When the last fire brought the world to naught.

Persistent in his naughtiness the louse
In the dean's broad wig set up a bawdy house.

The Black Widow

Her web a crisscross tangle, not precise
And symmetrical like that of the orb
   Spinner, she sits, uncertain of her eyes
But alert for movement, to rush and grab
At blundering intruders, her eventual prize

For patience. Black and sleekly silk,
Finer in texture than a satin glove,
She waits in darkness, while humans talk
In ignorance about her and will rave
With old tales told by a forgotten folk.

As often as not, the miniature male
Escapes her hunger, so her usual name
Is not justified: yet her venom will
In strength outdo the rattlesnake. Fame
Such as hers I would not like to spoil

By pointing out that only a few
Had died from her charge and anxious bite.
I roll her over with a pencil, admire below
The vermilion hour-glass and her eight
Slim legs, her polished, more than ebony, glow.

Remembering that she can lift
A weight far bigger than herself, I leave
Her in her unkempt web, a slung soft
Hammock across an opening above
The cattle, where flies soar to the loft.

And her perfection is enough to please
A Faubergé, whose craftsmen never
Contrived such delicacy as in those
Fine feeling legs; no matter how clever
The enameller, his purest or his rarest glaze

Could not repeat that gleaming black,
Nor mechanic with his cunning artifice
Make motion such as hers. A weak
Small spider, perhaps, yet in her place
Perfect for what she'd undertake.

The Farm, Early Morning

The cattle congregate
Beside the looming barn; a fog
Of breath distills in the frost-bound air.
Slowly light breaks the duck-egg
Sky. The chickens repeat

Their morning litany. Cat-ice
Slicks the pond's unruffled water,
And the still silence presses on the ear,
As if to say that now, or later,·
Motion in this place

Will harm the quiet.
But for this long moment I
Look through the mantilla of twigs here,
Crying halt to dawning day,
Enjoying my eyot

In spating time.
Now I am just a pair of eyes
Watching, and a sleeping mind aware
Of approaching winter days,
Of snow to come.

An Upper, Left Central, Incisor
for C.M.H.

This tooth, which came early to replace the childhood one,
Had suffered much—loosened boxing, cracked by a bull's
     feet,
Sideswiped by bomb-casing in Lamb's Conduit Street—
It was my familiar. But now, quite gently, it has gone.
Inelegant, perhaps, being crazed like aged Roman pottery,
Still, it was often tough enough to deal with any steak,
And I, eternally an optimist, had hoped it would not break
At the unforeseeable drawing of gastronomic lottery.

Oh, tooth, companion for thirty-five odd and curious years,
My extra hand, clipper of ends of thread and bits of string,
I shudder as I feel your neighbours shake; I share their fears
Of the bright mechanics that the future now must bring.
Suffering alone, I tongue your obvious, though healing,
     gap,
Lamenting, as perpetually, unwanted changes in a private
     map.

Garland for the Winter Solstice

The sun stands still and flowers
Are all withdrawn, but memories
Give back cardinal lobelia, tall
Scarlet fountains for the humming-bird—
Vined, broken with blue and liver apios—
Beside hanging horns of jewelweed,
With pods which pop when prodded
By the idle or enquiring finger.

Also remain those favourite swamps
Where calopogon, butterfly-winged orchid,
Flaunted its magenta above pink-
Tinged sphagnum and crimson sundew,
Black water in the mind has purple spires
Of pickerelweed, and sweetly odoured
Lilies, richly scattered, and yellow cups
Of spatter-dock stemmed on the mud.

Orange pompons of butterfly-weed
Brighten the bare expanse of memory,
Where also grow the milkweed,
With rubbery white sap and knobbly pods,
Short-flowering stars of blue-eyed grass,
And rather more persistent amaryllis—
Golden stargrass on untravelled roads—
And the too seldom glory of wood-lily.

Asters and goldenrod for autumn equinox,
With the blue wheels of chicory, and,

At all times, the dandelion, that plant
Which, having become perfect for purpose,
Has forsaken sex and can evolve no more;
Also, little ladies'-tresses in the tawny fields,
And, under various trees, the last red-flushed
Indian-pipe—ghost-flower or fairy-smoke.

Before next solstice, I shall see once more
The arethusa by the woodland paths,
The galaxy of violets, and wintergreen,
Round-leaved and creamy belled,
Skunk-cabbage poke up beside a stream,
Bluets, whose masses make up for lack
Of size, and meadows staring white
With ox-eye daisies, untamed chrysanthemums.

There will be slender blue flag by the swamp,
And saffron-stamened deergrass,
Lambkill and lady's-slippers in the wood,
And the wild rose with fragile petals.
The yellow thistle will rule sandy banks,
And the devil's-paint-brush will be obvious
Among the tombstones, a curious irony;
Swamps will have candles, Linnaeus' mistaken mistletoe.

Now, perched on this polar height
When all sap lies quiet and does not climb,
When all seems dead, I cultivate
The wild garden rioting in my memory,
Count in advance the treasures which
The sleeping sap contains, knowing that
Both alien and native will surely reappear
Regardless of my attentions and delight.

I see also that this deathlike sleep
Is only for a while. All is not interred
For bright scarlet partridge-berries
Shine among green and polished leather leaves,
And through the snow emerge
Umbrellas and spikes of strange club-moss,
And winter runs from now toward
The waking of the sap and spring.

The Eye

The eye, nimble as a rat,
Claims *droit de seigneur* with what it sees,
    Does not hesitate at rape,
    But thinks its bludgeon wit
Sufficient recompense, doled out to those
    Who suffer from its slap.

    The bouncing eye is thrifty
And banks all treasures it can catch
    So easily. It is a thief,
    Slick as a con, crafty
In depredation, weighing what it can snitch
    From independent life.

    The eye is fortunate
And has not been tried, or caught, as yet.
    The eye makes no apologies
    For being itself, profligate
And not to be stifled by the lawyer's writ,
    Or taken by surprise.

    The eye, pulled into court,
Would smirk and then blackmail the judge,
    For, being well aware
    Of movement, its subtle art
Would give it the opportunity in which to edge
    Its way out of the door.

Without the vanished eye,
Skipping and bottom-pinching, each one lost,
    Closed in his shade,
    Would have to cry,
'Oh, pardon the delinquent; wandered in mist
    I am alone, afraid.'

The Heifer Jacked

Stubborn, as calves are stubborn, she would refuse
To turn, unless it convenienced her; would wander
At will, convinced, it would seem, the lusher grass
Grew outside the gate. She would pause and meander
From tuft to tuft, unconcerned by the tag on her ear,
Or the label at her neck, held there with binder-twine.
She would lift an incurious head to gaze after a car
And return to her heiferish business, which was her own.

She was tame and would suck on an offered finger,
And would, if she could, run for her mother's milk;
When she moved, she moved with a suitable languor,
Befitting her pedigree and her coat slick as silk.
    But then, in a morning, she was suddenly gone
    To a care-nothing death, hunting anything brown.

A Maryland Vineyard

for C. & E.S.

Here, where the great grapes will not grow,
Where phylloxera destroys the famous vine,
Only the wind speaks of Sémillon and Pinot,
Only the memory recalls Riesling and the Rhine.

Where phylloxera destroys the famous vine,
And foxy labrusca used to sprawl,
Only the memory recalls Riesling and the Rhine;
Names have gone and numbers now rule all.

And foxy labrusca used to sprawl
Where hybrids grow which have no taint;
Names have gone and numbers now rule all,
Ravat's great two-six-two knows no restraint.

Where hybrids grow which have no taint,
New vines await the fruiting and the press;
Ravat's great two-six-two knows no restraint,
Bouquets are hidden that future years will bless.

New vines await the fruiting and the press;
Here, where the great grapes will not grow
Bouquets are hidden that future years will bless;
Only the wind speaks of Sémillon and Pinot.

Trout Flies

for J.K.M.

Ten years of age and intent upon a tea-brown burn
Across a moor in Lanarkshire, brass reel and greenheart
Rod, my first, I tried them out and came to learn
These magic names, from which I now can never part.

The insignificant ones were best, so ran the story
Of the old man who slowly taught me how to cast:
Dark Snipe, perhaps, Cow Dung, or favourite Greenwell's
  Glory,
Would attract the sleek trout that moved so fast

To attack and suck the right and only fly.
Gaudy Partridge & Orange could be used, he said,
By those who fished on lochs, *his* fish would shy
From bright Butcher, Cardinal, or Teal & Red.

Now, on a clear day, a Wickham's Fancy might
Deceive a hungry trout, or even a Red Spinner,
But Coch-y-Bondu, or March Brown, in failing light,
Were more certain to bring home the dinner.

Watching the dull fly settle gently on the water
I would await the tug and make my strike,
While these names became a permanent mortar
Between my memories, names that I like

And tongue familiarly, Black Midge and August Dun,
Blue Upright, Cinnamon Sedge, Coachman and Pheasant
 Tail,
Red Ant, Red Hackle, Furnace Palmer, and Yellow Sally,
 in the sun,
Ghost, Green Midge, Half Stone and, sometimes, Never
 Fail.

The Geese

Like a singed black lash, curled in the embers
Of the night, spiralling from opening day, the skein
Of Canada geese appears. Too distant for numbers
It seems one bar, half-hidden in the splintering rain.
Slowly, though, the surge of the great birds flying,
Ploughing invisible furrows in the morning air,
Brings them clear, distinct in the dawn's greying,
Curved wings thrashing, necks stretched before.

High, out of range of the skilled gunner's shot,
They circle, their honks borne faintly on the wind,
Inspecting the decoys with which the hunters plot
To bring them in. Dissatisfaction now will send
Them on, obedient to their vast leader's call—
A team of aerial swimmers beating out their crawl.

Laugharne Churchyard in 1954

Three thousand miles and nearly half a year
Away from a drab November afternoon, hysterics
Of friends forgotten, and also the plain derricks
Hoisting the grey coffin, I myself stand here

Savouring the early spring and Carmarthen mist,
Looking at humped soil and at the celandine
That grows on turned earth, flourishing between
Knotgrass and coltsfoot which the digger missed

While breaking clods. By the old stone wall
The primroses are showing, and on mud flats
The heron calls; the sea comes in, and rats
Gnaw at gifts the estuary brings them all.

This morning I walked with the gold-polled son
In search of imaginary cows, while bluebells
And violets distracted us, but all their smells
Were redolent of hospital. Suddenly I was one

Who thought of the death of him, my friend,
In a far country where he was a stranger, while
I knew it now as home. The child's bright smile
Reflected the father's face, the path would wend

Across his landscape, and the lonely crying birds
Yammered his background. Now, in this untidy
Churchyard, looking at sodden soil, I recall the mighty
Swell of that voice, the roll and thunder of words

In public places, but, more particularly, the bars
And friendly houses where we would meet and joke
About our situation, we, the perennially broke,
With, always, limericks and gossip about the stars

Of our own worlds, those whom success had loved.
Now, past the thin iron gates, past the wall-rue
And hart's-tongue, success, my friend, has taken you
To that country which another poet had already proved

A source for fabulous tales. Damp now, I shiver,
Take a last look at the awkward hump of earth,
Recalling that your funeral gave rise to mirth,
And turn away, knowing certainly that I will never

Again stand thus. Time and fame will neatly trim
This rubbish heap, and this grave itself become
A symbol of the poet in his long-sought home.
And I, forgetting this, carry my memories of him,

My jester, drinking companion, and old friend,
Sharer of careless youth and slapdash middle-age.
Records preserve his voice, his words are on the page
To prove that this drear mistiness is not the end.

Of Moulds and Mushrooms

Agrippina, well aware of Claudius' greed
For Caesar's mushroom, knew also that it looked
Like death-cap or destroying angel, so a god
Made room on earth for Nero, whose joke,
'Food of the gods,' allowed for deadly poison.

Some still, with unreasoning fear, disgust,
Kick or switch down the mushrooms by their path,
Leaving the amanita rudely shattered, gills
Like fallen feathers scattered, veil and volva
Broken, and all this symmetry destroyed.

The lack of chlorophyll suggests the parasite
Which guilty man so readily despises.
These are strange fruit of the thin mycellium,
That webs this world beneath the surface,
And which can persist in its invisibility

Breaking down discard of leaves and timber,
Which otherwise would overtop the wood
Extinguishing everything, so that the seed
May sprout to nourishment, and the cycle
Of death, decay and rebirth still go on.

And I, aesthetic and somewhat botanical,
Would note and praise the diversity
Of shapes, variety of colours of the fungi,
Ball, club, shelf, parasol, cup and horn,
And the suave velvet of the different moulds.

I would recall the fungi in their settings:
Fly-agaric, scarlet with wrinkled creamy warts,
In birch woods of Dumbartonshire, but lemon-
Yellow in New England, toxic they said to flies,
But intoxicant for the Kamchatka tribesman.

Near Selkirk once I found a monstrous puff ball,
Far bigger than my younger brother's head,
A gleaming baldpate beckoning me across the field
To find and greet poor Yorick's vegetable skull,
Solitary underneath the well-clipped hazel hedge.

Where anciently the monks had had their abbey,
Beside my Essex farmhouse, clustered blewits
Were palely violet below the dark-fruited sloes,
And the old gnarled oaks within the woods
Were sometimes richly shelved with beefsteaks;

And I, in a strictly rationed world,
Welcomed and ate these, and others that I found,
Spongy crèpe, chantrelle and honeycombed morel,
Grey oyster-mushroom and tall dignified parasol,
Which I again met later on a Chilmark lawn.

Brown-purple trumpets of the cornucopia
Stand clear against the brilliance of the moss
Under a clump of beech-trees at Gay Head,
While vast fairy-rings, some centuries of age,
Manacle the cropped grass of the South Downs.

The wooden ships of England knew dry-rot,
Pepys gathering toadstools bigger than his fists,
So that ten oaks were cut for each one used,
And the white-rimmed tawniness rioted again
Among the bombed buildings that I sometime knew.

Fungi have made their share of history:
St. Anthony's fire, from ergot in the rye,
Swept savagely through medieval France,
Rotting potatoes drove the Irishman abroad,
And French grapes grown on North American stock.

A mouldering cantaloup from a Peoria supermarket
Supplanted the culture Fleming kept for years,
And others now sample soil, remove and scan
The moulds that, in their destructiveness,
Aid ailing man by driving out his enemies.

But I, walking in fields or through the woods,
Welcome the vermilion russula, the sulphur
Polyporus, or inky shaggy-cap upon a heap of dung,
Without questioning their usefulness to me.
The ecology of my appreciation seems to need

Clavaria's coral branches on a damp dark bank,
Odorous stink-horns prodding through the grass,
And petalled dry geasters studding a sandy road.
These many-fangled fruits make bright
My sundry places where no flowers can bloom.

Sestina for Georges de la Tour

A patchwork of littleness is known about his life,
A quiet man living quietly in a lost provincial town,
Untouched by all the dazzling aspects of the court;
The diffused light reflected by the king as sun
Did not reach far enough to break into his night,
Illuminated only by a flaring torch or candle.

At dark, with bell and book and smoking candle,
He sought the ardours of the blessed life,
And worked with Franciscans in the dead of night
To start a flame burning in his own home town,
A small flicker to ask reference of the sun
But destined in time to light a fuse at court.

The Caravaggio so much admired at court
Was never his. His Sebastian lit by a candle
Was not Sebastian lying bloody in the sun
But merely a quiet body drained suddenly of life;
As quiet a death as any that his familiar town
Could lap in cerements on any given night.

While others knew the day, his mystic night
Knew more of splendour than any at the court.
Versailles was dull beside the treasure that his town
Could show him in the frail light of a candle:
His dark shadows made a sharp geometry of life
That was too often blurred by blaze of sun.

The state was Louis, and he was its sun
Whose glare was scarcely dimmed by any night;
The painter preferred the pattern of another life
To all the blandishments extended by the court.
His faith and brush could light so fierce a candle
It would burn farther than the confines of the town.

His vision, personal and controlled, made his town
Appear a place lost to the dazzlement of sun;
Warmed by the tepid heat of a weak wavering candle
He extended the boundaries of his private night
To trap reality that reached the lively court
With harsh reminders of lost actual life.

Not lonely in his town, he made the night
A time of brilliance, no sun blazing at the court
Compared with his dim candle, lighting a fringe of life.

Lament for Alpine Plants

'You can't get rock plants in France—alpine
flowers and so on.' The Duchess of Windsor,
quoted in the *New Yorker*, October 13, 1956.

The shy flowers wither on the mountainside,
Rock-rose and cyclamen have vanished from the screes,
Catchfly and Alpine flax defy the guide:

The saxifrage, which used to please
The climber, has gone with the dark columbine,
To other shades, other parts than these:

The lover of the gentian can repine
For it has gone, with windflower and meadow-rue,
Pink of Montpellier, azalea and orpine:

No longer can the hairbell's blue
Spread out a second sky scross an Alpine field,
Or butterwort have sticky dew.

Should, indeed, the Duchess wield
Words which were loaded with the slightest fact,
The plants might to her statement yield:

But flowers, although so sweepingly attacked,
Struggle to linger, each in its favoured place,
While other greener fingers, tipped with tact,
Mix some humility with all their grace.

The Hawk's Victim

I take the sandy path that goes
Across the moors: on this most bitter day
A rosette of fallen feathers shows
That a high hawk went hunting here;

And in this strange and winter landscape,
With dry leaves on huckleberry and bay,
The torn victim that did not escape,
Is brilliant suddenly, a flower's display.

I see the foliage in the wings,
That cup cheek-feathers and soft down,
As blossoms, but a gust flings
My fancy wide: so rudely blown

The feathers are only those of a dead bird,
And overhead the hunting hawk still swings.
Ignoring my fancy, so personal and absurd,
It scans the moors, to see what bareness brings.

Marginalia on a Letter of Keats

A bird of the suburbs is the Titmouse,
Snatching at suet suspended from a branch,
Building its nest within a man-made house;
Certainly no Cutty Wren for men to lynch.

A poet of the suburbs was John Keats,
Plucking at nature as hard as he was able,
Or struck astonished by older poets' feats;
Weaving a world where he became a fable.

A strange meeting when those two got together—
A minor duel that could but end in death—
That curious day when, in mating weather,
John Keats shot a Tomtit on the Heath.

Amphisbaenic Sonnet

Poke down drains, peer in the drawer,
Attack, smash down the chancel door,
Storm up the aisle, overthrow the rood:
No grail awaits you there as your reward.

When the light of early dawn unpeels
The darkness down to the last star,
You will find only the ravening rats
You dreamed of in your unquiet sleep.

Do as you like—you can never dam
The horror rising like a sullen tide
Until the bleeding brain is truly mad
With visions no one will ever edit.

Try to avoid the coming of this evil
By learning how to start to live.

Two-Legged Cat

Old dot-and-carry-two, Boots the cat,
Who lost one front and one back leg
To a hay-mower, is not put out by that.
Chased by no dog, he's grown sleek and fat
On veteran's rights, while others have to beg.

The Judgement of Fish

After the last echoing of the final trump, then,
They say, the seas will vanish or dry up, but first
These need attention: before justice comes to men
Fish must be weighed, the blessed and the cursed.

Before damned men come tumbling down, pell-mell,
Belly up, the sinful among fish must rise to hell.

Dream

In an enormous garden where the lavender
Hung in the air, tinting the fringes of the sun
With its pale hues, I stood and saw you there,
Hearing your voice trilling in a scale's run.

While the flickering notes continued to unwind,
You left: I heard only the gardener's shears
Snickering and clicking in the sullen wind
As they lopped off the scented bursting ears.

Then I saw you in a long corridor, again,
But between us crept a black cripple, held
By two grey guards, whose cuffed refrain
Drove the unprotesting to where I beheld

You, once more, standing by an open gate.
Then I stood outside, with thistle and cactus,
Kicking against the wall, knowing it late,
My death's head twitching in an uncertain rictus.

The Sea Horse

This sea horse, errant upon Sargasso weed,
Came on the tiny bladders to these colder shores,
Squirmed from the loaded scallop-dredge, slid
Among the clutter, being swept abruptly from the lairs
Of king-crab, conch and starfish, to collide

With an unassimilatable element. Its tail,
Prehensile, curled strongly round my finger,
A rigid band, harsh for one so very small,
As if its horror of the air had forced an anger
Against my hand, lying limply in the cull

Of broken shells and eel grass. Eyes were blue
Against its shiny black, and flexible armour
Was not crisp and brittle as in the dry
One before me on my table as I write here;
Recalling later the wonders of a world I hardly know.

This strange and amulet fish attracts
As no other, though it is true that man as male
Sheers from the brood-pouched stallion, rejects
A system which might make him also feel
The burdens of motherhood. These defects

In my imagination still cannot destroy
My appreciation of this so unfamiliar stranger,
Which, for a long moment, I held, let lie
Convulsive in my palm, then watched it linger
In reorientation before it twirled away

Upright in the water; dorsal fin as screw
Propelling it down to the eel grass and the mud
Where once more on its own errantry it could go,
Compelled by will or hunger, wish or need,
Driven through regions my man's eyes never saw.

Dead Owl

My hand, though competent, is inadequate to hold
   This screech-owl, killed by a car.
   Despite such encounters made before
Surprised, five limber fingers find they are unskilled
And cannot cope with this, a compact and a petty death.
   This owl, heard but not so closely seen
   Until this twilight, in this winter lane
I lifted casually from the stark snarls of undergrowth.

Eyes and hands sleek down the tousled feathers,
   Rim beak, stroke earlike tufts:
Mind hesitates, while the yellow evening gathers
   Calm before snow, then briefly sifts
Small sudden deaths from one another, but has qualms
And, human, cannot intrude in these, death's tinier realms.

Antipodes
for R.P.W.

Somewhere, under the bedrock of the world I walked,
Under the cling of clay, the sifting of sand,
If I dug far enough I chanced to find
My antipodes, where Maoris, unprovoked,
Would welcome me, where I would stand
As the mind's explorer, creator of worlds evoked.

There, I knew, by virtue of the grace of gravity,
I would walk upside down, a fly
Parading on the world's fat underbelly,
With the slick assurance of a deity
Come to inspect his sources of supply,
Benevolent, but with strict attention to his duty.

The holes which I would dig, with childish skill,
Could not go deep enough, mud
Collected or tumbling sand hid
Southern stars, the unpropped wall
Crumbled, while the adults said
New Zealand lay deeper than the deepest well.

My own antipodes, I came at last to realize,
Were human and not geographic,
Gravity was mental not specific,
And forever the digger's prize
Lay in the digging. Luck
Produced its antipodes beneath my very nose.